THAT WAS CLOSE!

Paul Wilson

ACKNOWLEDGEMENTS

All my friends and family for asking me to put these experiences together in a book.

My wife Leslie for her help in spelling and editing, especially the Glossary, using her experience as a Private Pilot and a qualified Aircraft Accident Investigator.

My daughter Creonne for her detailed and valuable editing of my scribbles.

My friend Captain Mike Trehan for showing me the way by writing his books "The Gift".

My friend Bob Lewis for his enthusiastic encouragement and help in arranging the publishing of the book.

Copyright © Flight Lieutenant Paul Wilson RAF (Rtd.) 2015
The right of Flight Lieutenant Paul Wilson to be identified as the author of this work has been asserted by him in accordance with the Copyright, Designs and Patents Act 1988.

Published by Paul Wilson

ISBN 978-0-9932479-0-3

Produced by The Letterworks Ltd, Reading

CONTENTS

Introduction	1
Chapter 1: Chipmunk	5
Chapter 2: Oxford	13
Chapter 3: Meteor Mk 7	17
Chapter 4: Metoeor Mk IV	19
Chapter 5: Meteor Mk 8	24
Chapter 6: Varsity	28
Chapter 7: Meteors Again	36
Chapter 8: Canberra	37
Chapter 9: Valiant B1	41
Chapter 10: Victor Mk 1	58
Chapter 11: Victor Mk 2	64
Chapter 12: Piston Provost	67
Chapter 13: Jet Provost	68
Chapter 14: Gnat	69
Chapter 15: Chipmunk, Again	81
Chapter 16: Boeing 707–436	85
Chapter 17: Concorde	87
Chapter 18: Boeing 720B	89
Chapter 19: Boeing 707–336	90
Chapter 20: Dragon Rapide DH 89	93
Chapter 21: TB 10 Tobago	94

*Dedicated to my late wife
Moira
Whose love and support gave me
strength to survive these events.*

Introduction

This is a book for people who have an interest in aviation. There is a motto known to Old Aviators that goes: "There are old pilots, and there are bold pilots – but there are no old, bold pilots!" Well, here I am writing this book! The book started out as simply memories of flying surprises but has turned into more of an autobiography.

I hope that will give more of an insight into why the events were special. The book is a record of some of the more interesting events in my flying career. They are trawled from memories of many years ago, and included because a number of my friends and colleagues thought it would be entertaining to read. After so long these events are all real enough to me but where others are involved their recall of the event may vary. When that is the case I welcome their comments and would enjoy reading, or hearing, what they remember of the event.

You don't have to be an aviator but understanding the jargon will allow you to share the joy and excitement of these memories better. There is an extensive glossary for the uninitiated at the back and I've tried to make it clear.

The chapters are by aircraft type in chronological order. I've also tried to keep the events on each aircraft in chronological order, where I have put a comment in my Log Book. Members of the Basic Flying Training Course that I attended were only given Log Books at the end of the Course. We then transcribed our flying times to our Log Books from a collection of Log Sheets used on a daily basis. So, I was never one to keep notes or photos as a record in my Log Book.

My Log Books have a variety of methods of recording information. Night Flying was seen as rather an unusual event when I was learning to fly and was therefore entered in red pen! There is a description of such events in the Chapter on the Chipmunk. Instrument flying was seen as a necessary evil and was recorded separately because each hour accumulated to various thresholds. At each threshold a more difficult Instrument Flying Test was passed to be allowed to fly in a worse set of meteorological conditions. Simulated Instrument Flying, in a Link Trainer[1], was initially regarded with suspicion and recorded separately to real flying.

---

[1] The Link Trainer Fig. 3. was an enclosed cockpit set on a universal joint and wobbled about in response to the controls operated by the pilot interpreting blind flying instruments. See Glossary for more.

Some of these events may seem highly dangerous and a bit wild, but it was a long time ago and life was very different then. I would probably make the same mistakes all over again if I relived the past. Veterans may see some of this as "Shooting a Line", as bragging was known, but to them I would say; "This is my memory of events recorded in my Log Book". Equally, some of my colleagues and supervisors did not like my style of flying which was to operate in an innovative way not necessarily covered by the rules or conventions, but it got the job done. However, some of them ended their flying career as "holes in the ground" and I'm writing this book.

I was privileged to be one of the first pilots to fly a number of aircraft on their introduction into the RAF. I even managed to fly one factory aircraft before it was released to the RAF for Squadron Service. Four of the aircraft in the book I flew before the RAF had issued the Pilots Notes for the type.

Some of you may wonder why there is no mention of the precise location of these events. While still serving in the RAF I submitted a manuscript describing some of these events that I hoped to publish and was told not to include locations that could be identified. This book has been written with that requirement fulfilled.

AN INTEREST IN AIRCRAFT

For some reason Wilson parents have an urge to name their sons Paul. There seem to be every other male Wilson with this name so I do not have any claim to fame through my name. Thus, I have a type of anonymity as I merge into this crowd of Paul Wilsons. I was born in 1931. As an only child, with a doting mother and a father who despaired at trying to discipline me, my early years were amongst mostly adults.

At the age of about three and a half my parents took me to Shoreham Airport. We were watching "Alan Cobham's Flying Circus" and I was very impressed. The Public Address system was describing the flying and was interrupted with a message. "Will the parents of the child climbing into the aeroplane across the runway please prevent him from doing any damage". My mother turned to my father and said: "What a disgrace! Letting a child run off like that. – Where's Paul – oh my God – go and get him". I decided then that flying was what I wanted to do. I did manage to achieve all the flying targets I set myself, although some were only fleetingly enjoyed.

It is surprising how memory filters the nuggets of significant events into a neat package of outstanding importance, a bit like swirling the mud in a gold panning tin when suddenly the shining morsels of gold are discovered. Some of the events stored amongst my golden bits are of a sharpness honed by emotion – but I digress!

AIRCRAFT WITH RADAR

My father worked with "the wireless"[2] as the new medium of mass communication and entertainment was called in the 1930s. Jobs were difficult to find but his expertise was such that we moved around the country to different accommodation during my childhood. This lead to his interest in the world's first Television sets that came into use in the London area. He became skilled at diagnosing faults and repairing them, as well as selling them, as manager to a retail chain shop. Because he had been involved with television, when the war came, my father was recruited to work for the Air Ministry on servicing and developing airborne radar. So, we went to live close to the aerodrome where he worked and I could watch the aeroplanes to my heart's content.

HARD LESSONS

At first the aircraft were mainly of Coastal Command, with strange antennae on the wings and fuselage. These Aerials were the original U–Boat[3] hunting radar called ASV, Air to Surface Vessel. The aircraft were mostly Ansons, Wellingtons and Hudsons and the Hudsons had some spectacular crashes on landing. They almost always caught fire on crashing and I discovered later that the undercarriage would punch a hole in the wing fuel tanks on crash landings. This allowed fuel to spill onto the hot engines and the whole thing rapidly became an inferno from which some of the chaps didn't get out. I decided that was a death I would not want – something that came back to haunt me later in my career.

ADOLESCENCE AND SCHOOL

Teenagers had not been invented in the 1940s but adolescent behaviour was much the same. Because we had moved around the countryside so much I had not attended school very much. When at last we settled, my mother had selected a school for me that unbeknown to her was for "slow"

---

[2] Now known as Radio.
[3] German submarines were known as U–Boats from the German Unterseeboot.

children, as they were called then. When the results of intelligence tests, these were equivalent to the Eleven Plus examination used later, were declared the Headmaster made a great fuss. My I.Q. turned out to be well into the bracket to go up to the premier senior school. Fortunately for me he made it happen – a valuable turning point in my life thanks to his recognition and actions.

In the Academy I struggled at first, because I did not have the foundations that the others had been given in previous years. However, not only did I pass the exams but was Head Boy of my House, a Prefect and Captain of the Gymnastic Team.

I had been a "sickly" child often suffering from bouts of bronchitis and not very strong. My life changed when I discovered a "Health and Strength" club near my home. Weight training, boxing and gymnastics gave me energy and ability that startled my mother! During the same time, as well as this training for Gymnastic Displays, I was going to Night Classes to study Wireless Theory at City and Guilds[4] level and Amateur Radio. I even found time for some Amateur Dramatics as well as doing my school homework. All this gave me a fairly "rounded" set of abilities that stood me in good stead when I arrived in the RAF.

Some of you may wonder why I do not have many photographs of the aircraft that I flew, with me in the foreground. Well, when I flew them they were so secret that photography in and around them was not permitted. Pity, but I've trawled around to get some representative illustrations.

---

[4] Standards set by the organisation for qualifications ranging from Apprentice to Postgraduate by the City of London.

Chapter 1

Chipmunk

First flown 9th February 1951

THE FIRST FLIGHT

Having joined the Royal Air Force late in 1950, as a National Serviceman, the first few months as an Airman were taken up with marching, drilling and handling a rifle and bayonet. Some more lessons in the science of flying and associated sciences followed and I was introduced to the Officers Mess, as a Cadet. To my disappointment members of subsequent Courses were given the privilege of being Acting Pilot Officers – but that's life!

The great day had come. After hours of Ground−school, days of marching and drill, I was at last in a cockpit. It was now 1951! I was issued with a brand new "flame−proof" flying suit, a leather helmet and oxygen mask that smelled of rubber. Attached to the helmet was that large electrical connector on the end of the wires that would connect me to the intercom[5] and radio. All these gave me a feeling that I had "arrived"! This was where I wanted to be.

The Chipmunk Fig. 1. was the first RAF training aircraft to have a closed canopy over the two pilots, sitting one behind the other. It was a low wing, fixed undercarriage with tail−wheel, metal and fabric, single−engine, fully aerobatic with two position flaps. Sitting behind me, my Flying Instructor had thoroughly briefed me on the purpose of the flight: "to experience the effect of the flying controls on the aircraft".

The Instructor started the Chipmunk, taxied out to the runway and we were rolling for take−off. The grass was bumpy and the canopy rattled as we gained speed. Then all was smooth, the roaring engine and the beckoning blue sky meant the waiting was over. At last out there, waiting for me, was the experience of my first flight – ever. We climbed up towards some puffy white clouds, then turned away and levelled off by throttling back to a cruising, less angry, roar of the engine.

The Instructor talked to me as he showed how the aircraft banked from moving the control stick to the side and the rise and fall of the nose with the back and forward movement of the stick – always watching the horizon to see the amount of aircraft movement. My head filled with the blackboard diagrams of lift, drag and vector diagrams changing with bank angle. At least that had taught me that you don't steer an aeroplane with rudder. You just tilt the wings by banking and the imaginary big arrows (remembered from blackboard illustrations) Fig. 28. that poke up to keep you flying, tilt over to the side and drag you round the turn! To make sure we always knew who was flying the aircraft the phrases "I have control" or "you have control" were used.

[5] Voice communication within the aircraft.

Another landmark! The Instructor said "you have control. Show me a turn to the left." I grasped the stick whacked on about 80 degrees of bank and pulled the stick sharply back. We hit what I later learned was the Stall Buffet (a great shaking and banging of the whole aircraft) and, with a shriek of "I have control", the Instructor levelled the wings and brought the aircraft back into equilibrium.

He was not a Happy Chap and I was suitably chastised and encouraged to stroke the controls and watch the horizon diligently when performing, always gentle, manoeuvres. Years later when I had graduated to become an Instructor, and had taken my place in the back seat of a Chipmunk, I had a phrase I used to my Students: "Listen, you are designed to live in a tree but this aeroplane is designed to fly! Leave it alone and it will fly nicely. You only have to poke it when you want to change direction."

It took me some time to learn that because my early instructors failed to get through to me. Much later after I had been flying sorties lasting several hours at a time, I was gripping the controls tightly throughout a flight until someone pointed out to me the aeroplane would trim[6] and fly without my constant stranglehold!

SOLO

It was a beautiful June afternoon. Tufts of cotton wool like clouds floated in a sky that turned from distant grey to a deep blue overhead. A slight wind rippled the fabric of the wings of some Chipmunks but a shimmer of heat drifted up from the shiny metal fuselages. Three were lined up into the wind on the tufted field at the top of a slight hill.

Lying on the ground, waiting for my turn to fly, I could not see the far boundary fence of this field that shrank so much when seen from the cockpit in the air. Other Chipmunks roared away into the wind and sky. Later they would return, spluttering and swishing as they drifted overhead, descending to bounce friskily to a halt as they landed in the middle of the field. They shuddered and roared as the swished their tail taxiing back to dispersal[7] looking like some nervous insect. There I lay, head on my parachute, waiting for my Instructor.

He was one of several I had flown with, in the month or so that I had been flying. This one was a lanky red haired Scot with a bris-

---

[6] To trim was to use secondary flying controls to take any pressure off the hands and feet of the pilot.
[7] An area of the airfield set aside to park aircraft – dispersed from the main hangars.

tling moustache and a fine taste in moth eaten sports jackets. He came scrambling out of the low wooden hut which, although abandoned several times, now served as a time-keeper's office. Down at the other end was a larger room to keep students away from the Instructors. They needed the segregation to maintain some semblance of sanity after an hour shut up in a red hot flying greenhouse with an idiot student!

"Come on Lad…" he pointed, "…that one". "In you get and I'll do the outside check". I queried, "What are we off to do?" – "Circuits and Bumps this time" he replied, as I strapped on my parachute and got ready to climb into the front seat. Clambering in, I busied myself getting my 'chute' comfortable and my safety harness adjusted. Pulling on my helmet I thought "Don't forget to plug in or you won't be able to hear the 'Man in the Back'", and remember the radio call-sign is 'Beadle Charlie'!"[8]

I was still putting in the plug when I felt the Instructor climb in, 'dunt' me on the head and shout, "OK Start her up now". I got the troublesome plug fixed just in time to grab the hood as the Ground Crew chap slid it forward before he jumped off the wing. He waved a grubby thumb at me and ran round to the front of the aircraft. Another 'thumbs up' from the chap out front; but I'm not ready to start yet! I was still checking the flying controls, checking the various dials on the panel and doing the Pre-flight checks for starting – fuel, ignition switches, brakes and throttle, all at the same time! I found I was beginning to sweat slightly and to curse under my breath as I chanted the checks. "Swouff!" went the sudden noise in my headset. I jumped as this snort announced that the Instructor was now on intercom. I shouted to the ground-crew in front of us "Clear – start up". Thumbs up from the chap in front and I pulled the cord on the cartridge starter – Bang, Swish, Great Shudder, a touch more throttle and the engine settled down to a gentle tick over, with normal oil pressure.

The Man in the Back grunted, "Done the checks?"
"Yes Sir"
"OK I have control"
"Roger[9] Sir"

The chocks were waved away and we began to move forward, like a frightened salmon with tail swishing from side to side. Stabs of rudder and throttle allowed

---

[8] That would identify us to Air Traffic Control on the radio.
[9] Roger, was a code word meaning "message received and understood".

us to see each side of the nose looming up in front hiding the path ahead.
"Tower from Beadle Charlie, Taxi"
"Beadle Charlie – clear taxi – Queen Fox Easy[10] one, zero, one, five – Runway 05" "Beadle Charlie" As the Instructor swished our way across the field from dispersal to Runway 05, I was busy setting the pressure reading on my altimeter to 1015 and checking it read zero feet. He lined us up at right angles to the take-off direction and said "Right Oh Laddie, you have her. Do your checks and she is all yours". I had stopped sweating so much now as I ran up the engine to check for any fall in revs as I switched between magnetos. While doing that I had run through the pre-take-off checks in my head. I now chanted them aloud for the Instructor as I completed them, "… Hood shut, Harness tight, that's it – ready to go Sir".
"Right, now I want you to do a normal take-off, climb straight ahead to circuit height, 1000 feet, then turn downwind ready for a landing – OK? The "circuit" pattern, the rectangular path flown from take-off to landing, was climb ahead and turn cross wind climbing to 1000 feet, then turn downwind and fly until opposite the end of the runway, turn cross wind until turning onto finals to line up with the runway on the final descent to land.
"Roger Sir"
"Beadle Charlie take-off?"
"You're clear to go, Charlie" replied the Tower
"Charlie Roger" All very relaxed!

    A quick look up the approach to see if there was anything coming – then release the brakes and turn into wind. Gently open the throttle up to full power keeping her running straight with rudder, check RPM and oil pressure– speed building, tail up, bump, bump we're off! The rattling hood gave way to a smooth climb with speed building and the nose up above the horizon where it should settle on the climb. As I was trimming the Instructor said "That was OK. Now watch your climbing speed". I thought "what is he so worried about we're going up – aren't we?" "Roger Sir". We climbed up to our 1000 feet and turned Downwind I called the Tower "Downwind" and chanted the Downwind Checks, Vital Actions[11], as I did them. The Man in the back suddenly said "Turn in now" "Roger", I turned in and cut the power. The engine roar was replaced by a gentle spluttering

---

[10] This was the three letter code used as a sort of shorthand to give the air pressure on the airfield. When set on the Altimeter it would read zero. In the air, you then knew how high you were from the ground at the airfield. [11] The checks done by a pilot before take-off or landing to ensure that the aircraft configuration was correct. They were done to a mnemonic for each occasion which fitted all aircraft types at the time.

"Charlie Finals." The Tower responded "You're clear to land Charlie" "Roger", that's the field coming up nicely, I'm going to be just to the left of that other Chipmunk. The Instructor now began to talk me through the landing, "Watch your speed now –don't put the rest of your flap down yet or you'll undershoot OK put it down now − watch that other chap − check back now, you're a bit fast − let it float − check!" The Chipmunk settled onto the bumpy grass, jumped and rattled as it slowed down. "I have control" said the Man in the Back as he opened up the engine and he took us back into the circuit, talking as we went. "That's OK now, just a shade fast. Don't look over the nose so much, look out sideways, just in front of the wing. You can judge your height better on the last round out and touch." He turned onto the Downwind leg and said "OK you have control". Through the checks and the radio calls I went again − turn onto Finals, cut the power − speed just right − going down into the field nicely.

"Where's that flap lever" − Damn! My glove is caught − that's the flap lever down, at last! "CHECK", came the shout from the back BOMP, THE MAIN WHEELS HIT THE GROUND! "I have control". The engine roared and without touching the turf again we began to climb away. "What are ye doing Laddie − you'll kill us all! You must not look over the nose. You flew us straight into the ground then; there would have been an almighty thump if you hadn't checked when I told you". My glove had come free, I don't know when. I was sweating again thinking, "For goodness sake stop binding (the RAF word for moaning) and let me fly the thing − he's not in a very happy state of mind today. I'll never get rid of "The Man in the Back!".

In silence we turned Downwind and he went through the checks. Then came, "She's all yours now − land her". "Roger", silence again! It was a peach of a landing, all three points kissed the ground together and we stopped almost at once. "I have her" he said as we stopped.

In silence we turned out of wind and he went through the after landing checks before he taxied. We began to return to dispersal. "Well, I made a muck up of that little lot!", I thought to myself. Still the last one was good. "Do you want to go off now?" came from the back.

"Off?", I queried.

"Yes − on your own − how do you feel about going solo now?"

"I think − It's a good idea!"

"Right − Beadle Charlie going solo now".

The tower replied, "Roger Charlie". They would keep a sharp eye on Beadle Charlie!

The Instructor climbed out onto the wing and leaned into the rear cockpit to set it up for solo flying. Switches set to the front cockpit and harness tight so as not to float about. "You're sure you're OK?" He stood there on the wing, head forward and leaning against the slipstream of the idling engine. "Ready to go, Sir", I bellowed, but a shiver of excited sweat ran down the small of my back. The hood closed and the Instructor was gone. What was it that he had said? Go off – do a couple of turns around the field and then land. So this was IT! Now it's time to do some serious before take–off checks. Better do them again just to make sure! "Beadle Charlie, take off".

The tower simply responded, "Clear to go Charlie".

"Charlie Roger" I replied as I looked up the approach to see it was clear. Brakes off and into wind we go, throttle gently open to full. Twitch of the rudder to hold straight as the tail comes up.

Rattle – Bump – Bump – Airborne!

"Watch that climbing speed".

"Yes Sir".

What's that! There's nobody in the back. Not the back cockpit but in the back of my head! As I reach 1000 feet, throttle back to cruise around the field. There's the Instructor standing smoking a cigarette by the windsock. "Watch your airspeed" "Yes Sir". There it is again! It must just be the habit of hearing him telling me, even when I could see it happening for myself! It was as if he was looking over my shoulder, but there's nobody in the back this time! "Sing me a Happy Song", I sang to myself and rocked the wings, just feeling good at being up there all by myself, at last. The hot air lifted and bounced us about, the plane and me. I let it sway and corrected. I let it drift into a turn and then snapped it back, round the other way then steepening the turn, just the plane and me! No one to say turn this way or that – turn which way? I looked down to find I had strayed from the field. But, I could see it not too far away so I headed back.

"Charlie Downwind" – positioning myself as accurately as I could.

"Charlie clear Finals" came back the reassuring voice of the Tower.

"Charlie, Roger", and I went through the checks. It takes time to fly all the Downwind leg so I just did the checks again!

Time to turn in on the field, round we go and cut the power to a spluttering idle. Airspeed good, "Charlie Finals"
"Clear to land Charlie"
"Roger", now let's get this right.
Watch your speed now – don't put the rest of the flap down yet, you'll undershoot – OK put it down – watch that other character – check back now to keep the speed right – don't look over the nose, look in front of the wing – check BOMP, rattle and we rolled to a stop.
"Charlie, clear complete", I called as I turned crosswind. Now, checks after landing and we waddle back to dispersal, looking alternate sides of the nose. Wow, that was a peach of a landing, all three wheels together. I could hear that voice from the back just as if he had been sitting there! I had heard it so many times I think he talked me down very well. Looks like there is no escape, but that is no bad thing – he knows how to get it done right!

GETTING THE HANG OF THE CONTROLS

Those first few hours after going solo are always memorable for a pilot. Getting the feel of the controls and feeling the effects of speed and being inverted. Whizzing around the little cumulus clouds, following the contours of cloud – if you get it wrong you only hit the cloud, so no harm done. Trying the first Barrel Roll and finding when you're inverted that you don't have enough bank and rudder. So you finish with a half loop and are glad you started the manoeuvre at a height that gave you enough space to get back straight and level. After a while there was no longer a need to think where to place the flying controls, just look out of the aircraft and decide which direction to go and the muscle memory moved the controls until you were off in that direction.
Even if you were "looking up" at fields and countryside the new found coordination and orientation together made controlling the aircraft a joy to experience.

FIRST NIGHT FLYING

Another first was the occasion of night flying. The runway was marked out with "gooseneck flares". Fig.22. These were small oil filled cans with a long extension on one side that had a wick poking out. It looked rather like a watering can with flame coming out instead of water. The wick fed oil to the flame which flickered at the end. There were about five of these in a single line, into wind on the grass. These goosenecks were the original lighting for a runway at night and "flare−path"[12] became the generic term for a lighted runway. At the up wind end were two more flares on either side at right angles to the flare−path. It seems a bit primitive today but you have to remember that only a few years before in WWII chaps were landing in France by the light of electric torches. Landing lights were not used but there was a line of dim battery driven blue lights from the Apron, the concrete aircraft park next to the hangars, to the flare−path. We took off on the left side of the flares and landed on the right side. As students this was only attempted on fairly calm nights with good visibility and we didn't leave sight of the runway.

Another problem that we learned to overcome was that of the errors in the Flight Instruments. The Artificial Horizon[13] was the main instrument in the middle of the panel and showed the aircraft attitude. This suffered from particular errors when accelerating and climbing on take−off. If the wings were kept level on that horizon and the pitch indications used, the flight path became a diving turn into a hole in the ground! This had been discovered by Spitfire pilots, early in WWII, where the effect was much greater because of the greater acceleration. The basic instruments had to be monitored carefully and the Artificial Horizon disregarded until un−accelerated flight was regained.

However, the most exciting part was that at the time it was a requirement for all aircraft to be flown on an airtest by day before night flying! This gave the more adventurous Instructors a chance for low level aerobatics over the airfield − which we all enjoyed watching. And, in my case, flying in the back for the experience.

---

[12] A line of Gooseneck Flares Fig.23 showing the runway.
[13] A horizontal line across the instrument Fig. 25. represented the horizon and moved to stay level when the aircraft moved.

Chapter 2

Oxford

First flown 21st June 1951

NOW FOR WINGS

Having graduated from Basic Flying Training School flying Chipmunks I was posted to fly Oxfords. On these I would gain my "Wings" or RAF Flying Brevet.

UNINSPIRING ...

The Oxford Fig.5. was a 1930s design and had been around in the RAF as a trainer and communications aircraft since before the Second World War. There was a place for two Pilots, side by side each with full flight instruments, with other seats behind. These seats could be used for Signallers or Navigators but these were not in use when training Pilots. With twin engines it had no feathering[14] mechanism on the propellers which made it quite difficult to fly on one engine. By "feathering" a propeller the blades were turned into and not across the airflow when the engine stopped, thus reducing the drag and turning moment on that engine. The Oxford had the smell of high octane aviation fuel, doped fabric stretched over a wooden frame, and low pressure hydraulic fluid – a set of most evocative smells to an aviator of the era.

At this era of aviation the first thing to be done was to sit in the cockpit and memorise where all the switches and dials were located. With two engines there seemed to be an enormous array of dials and switches after the simple cockpit of the Chipmunk. The test was to sit in the cockpit blindfolded and then point to, or touch, any switch or dial called by your Instructor! The flight instruments were the same, and in the same layout on the panel, as the Chipmunk. This was a standard layout set by the RAF in the 1930s.

Up until the 1930s various instruments were set around the front of the cockpit and the pilot used them as he wished to keep the aircraft "right way up" and fly in the direction he chose. This random distribution of instruments was different for each aircraft type and sometimes each individual aircraft. This made it difficult for the pilot to coordinate the various bits of information into a picture of what the aircraft was doing.

The various sense organs for balance in the human frame were of no use and even produced false indications of motion so had to be disregarded while gathering the information from the instruments.

---

[14] Feathering used a mechanism on the propeller that could be operated when the engine was shut down to place the blades end on to the airflow.

The real breakthrough was the Artificial Horizon that had a bar across a circular instrument that could represent the real horizon, thus showing the attitude of the aircraft. Before that was introduced the attitude had to be inferred from combining separate bits of information from other instruments. The RAF used the artificial horizon as the main instrument and distributed the other instruments around it with them always being in the same pattern. The pilot could scan the instruments in a way that was always the same and could assimilate the information much more easily. This "Blind Flying Panel" later became a standard throughout the world. Fig.21.

To practice Instrument Flying there were amber coloured screens fitted in the windscreen and side panels and the pilot would wear blue tinted goggles. Through the goggles the instruments could be seen but the combined amber and blue stopped the pilot from seeing out of the cockpit. This system was known as "Two Stage Amber" and supplemented instrument flying in the Link Trainer, which was not nearly as realistic a machine as today's Flight Simulators.

I also learned that the mnemonic used for pre-takeoff and pre-landing checks was universally used on all RAF aircraft. It covered all the flying controls, all basic systems and included the more complex systems of advanced aircraft. Even today they can be used as a "Safety Net" when using multi-paged checklists on modern aircraft.

The Oxford was also not aerobatic so I was destined to get my wings by most of my flying being "right way up" and no chance to be upside down again for some time. However, it at least had a retractable undercarriage and hydraulic flaps! A number of my contemporaries were to fly Harvards that were single engine fully aerobatic aircraft. But, that was the luck of the draw and I was happy just to have an aircraft to 'play with', provided by the RAF.

... BUT CHALLENGING

However, the Oxford was a demanding aircraft to land with all three wheels touching together, as it had a tail wheel and could "swing" and veer off from the centre line of the runway very easily. Often it was easier to land by putting the main wheels on first before letting the tail down, but the "three pointer" was what I strived for when I could.

I soon discovered that when an engine was "failed" by my Instructor to test my ability to fly on one engine (asymmetric flight, as this was known technically) a practical solution was needed. It was no use filling your head with blackboard scribbles of aerodynamic vector diagrams and rudder angles. Just get a grip of the controls, especially the rudder, and fly the aircraft by instinct to make it stay straight and level. Your legs would soon let you know which engine had failed, because one was sticking out in front of the other to hold the rudder against the good engine. It was salutary training which served me well because I flew only multi-engine aircraft operationally, even the fighters, until towards the end of my RAF career.

AN EXCITING NIGHT FLIGHT

One of my most exciting trips was a night cross country flight towards the end of my "Wings" Course. I was not feeling well at the Briefing with a very heavy cold giving a runny nose and eyes. Some of my fellow course members helped me to finish the map and calculations before I staggered off into the air. I got up to cruising altitude and wandered around the route, managing to find all the turning points successfully.

The problem struck when I started the descent back to Base. Almost immediately there was a searing pain in the front of my head – I shouted aloud and screwed my eyes closed to overcome the pain. I realised that it was the change in pressure as I descended that was the problem so I applied power and climbed back up to cruising altitude. I still had my eyes almost closed but could just squint at the airspeed to ensure I didn't stall the aircraft. I called ATC and told them the problem and they called the Medical Officer to the Tower. I tried all the remedies suggested, holding my nose and blowing, trying to pop my ears and the like, but nothing cured the pain. There was no solution so I would just have to find a way to keep my eyes as open as I could and find the runway as best as I could. The descent and approach were excruciating and I could hardly see where I was going, concentrating on getting the airspeed right while lining up with the runway. I got down without mishap and then off to Sick Quarters for steaming menthol under a towel to try to clear my sinuses. I then understood how aircraft could just disappear with no trace, because I could well have just become out of control and crashed at any time on the descent. That was close!

WINGS

During this era in the RAF, the Officers Mess could be a fairly rowdy place. All manner of games involving feats of strength, balance and innovative ability were played, particularly after Dining In Nights. It was not unusual for some damage to be done to bits of the Mess and furniture. The usual penance after such events was a levy on everyone's Mess Bill, by the President of the Mess Committee (the PMC), of one day's pay. This spread the load of payment between the higher and lower ranks more evenly than a blanket charge. There was just such an evening the day before the parade for presentation of our wings. A rowdy series of rather drunken games ended with me being carried off the Sick Quarters with a busted ankle! So, I watched the Wing's Parade sitting with my parents and girlfriend, Moira later to be my wife! As my classmates marched off the Squadron Commander tapped me on the shoulder from behind, I turned and he handed me my wings. "You'd better have these", he said. Never mind, it had been a good party.

Chapter 3

Meteor Mk 7

First flown 7th January 1952

NOW A REAL AEROPLANE

The Mk.7 Fig.8. was the two seat trainer for the Meteor fighters that were the first jet aircraft to be operated by the R.A.F. As you can see from the Mark number 7, there had been many single seat Meteors before the trainer version was pressed into service. Many of the fighter pilots who converted onto this twin engined jet had no experience of flying a twin engined aircraft on one engine and found it a bit daunting. Having graduated for my Wings on the Oxford, that was a twin piston, I found no problems with the flight with one engine shut down on the Meteor. Having said that, it was not an easy aircraft to handle 'on one' (as it was known) because of the very high forces on the rudder pedal to hold straight even at cruise power. There was also the "phantom dive" which was a diving turn into the ground from the Downwind leg. If, when on one engine going Downwind in the Circuit, the air-brakes were left out when in the landing configuration the aircraft was sensitive to slip and skid and, if not balanced, the aircraft would 'depart'(roll upside down and dive down) into the ground.

FIRST JET FLIGHT

This aircraft was a quantum jump from the ancient Oxford and felt like the spaceships in the contemporary Boy's Magazines. On my introductory flight I was so amazed by the take-off performance that I was savouring the moment and watching the local scenery flash by when I suddenly realised the Instructor was calling my name. He had been saying my name several times to see if I was alright before I heard and responded. He was glad to hear that I was enjoying the experience and had never had any airsick experiences!

A NEW WAY OF LIFE

Up at 35,000 feet, unpressurised and living on 100% oxygen and in a freezing cockpit was to become a new way of life. Although some piston engine fighters had come up against the "Sound Barrier" on occasions, every time you flew a Meteor it was going to be close. If you let the aircraft go too fast or if you pulled too much G[15] in a tight turn you could be out of control and tumbling down into the thicker air, where the Mach Number[16] decreased, and you regained control.

---

[15] Even when turning in a car you can feel the forces on your body and in aircraft the force is much greater. It is expressed in multiples of the Force of Gravity at the surface of the earth when stationary – 1G. At about 3G some pilots start to lose consciousness as the blood can no longer be pumped to their brain. Figs. 26. & 28.

[16] A decimal number as a proportion of the speed of sound.

At this stage of flying high speed and high G skirmishes with the Barrier were all part of regular training. That way you came to know the feel of the controls as they changed with the approach to the Barrier and could avoid an embarrassing loss of control.

Another important lesson taught early in Meteor training was how the throttles required quite delicate control, especially at high altitude. At 35,000 feet the instructor said "I'm going to demonstrate the effect of mishandling the throttles. You hold the port throttle very firmly while I operate the starboard." I held on tight to the throttle and the Instructor whacked the starboard throttle fully open – the starboard engine coughed and we had a flameout[17] ! The engine just stopped immediately. This was another salutary lesson that I never forgot and applied to even the more advanced, and more forgiving, jet engines that I flew.

---

[17] The engine had stopped, no flame to keep the engine going.

Chapter 4

Meteor Mk IV

AT LAST, A FIGHTER TO FLY

First flown 29th January 1952

The Meteor was the RAF's first jet aircraft and this was the Mk IV. Fig.7. This was a fighter with two jet engines, to operate in the stratosphere and near the "Sound Barrier". It offered many new flying experiences, such as the regular training to approach that Sound Barrier and discover the change in the handling of the Flying Controls. Climb as high as the aircraft would go then nose down at full power and let the speed and Mach Number gradually increase. Too fast and the aircraft became uncontrollable, tumbling down into the lower and thicker air where those effects reduced to a controllable degree again.

These challenges made this new flying feel like I imagined those faced by the Science Fiction heroes I had read about as a small boy, and I revelled in the challenge. Quite often the whole of a 20 minute flight would be conducted above a sheet of cloud. The only radar available then was for the control of operational fighters so students were on their own navigation. On our maps were all the RAF stations that had radio direction finding kit so we could get bearings from them and that was what we used. It was made a bit more difficult because the Directional Gyro on the instrument panel would spin uncontrollably when doing aerobatics. To stop that doing damage we clamped it with the setting knob! So, before aerobatics I would fly so that the sun was on a wing-tip, note the direction, and then clamp the Directional Gyro, then do the reverse when it was time to return to Base. The ultimate bit of navigation was to stay silent on the radio throughout a 20 minute flight on exercise until time to get a bearing from the Base direction finder. You then asked for a bearing and were told that it signified that you were overhead the station! That was a good test of navigation ability. It was during such an attempt that I found I was going at a ridiculous speed over the ground in an Easterly direction. I gave up trying to navigate and got a Homing[18] back to Base, landing a bit short of fuel. That was my introduction to the effects of the Jet-stream, and we had aircraft scattered all over the country having got a bit lost on that day. The Met Man at the next morning briefing "waxed lyrical" over this newly discovered phenomenon and it was a great lesson in Meteorology.

As most of our flying was above the sheet of cloud, the first few times were a little daunting for the navigation but the real surprise was as you descended returning to base. As you hurtled down and met the top of the cloud sheet you didn't notice your shadow until as you entered the top of cloud

---

[18] A series of bearings, or headings, to follow bringing you gradually back to Base.

the shadow smacked into your aircraft! It was as if another aircraft suddenly appeared and whacked into you – but you did get used to that happening.

A FATEFUL DAY

The parachute that I carried slung over my right shoulder was awkward as I gripped the leather flying helmet in my left hand. As I walked towards the line of shiny silver Meteor aircraft parked side by side on the apron I looked up into the clear blue sky and the decision was made. Today everything was right, there was not a cloud over the British Isles, calm and predictable winds and an early slot on the flying programme. The sun was still low in the sky, even for autumn, so the aircraft was cold; my fingers were cold through the silk inners and cape leather gloves. My helmet was cold and greasy from the Brylcreem[19] and the cold unyielding oxygen mask smelled of rubber and sweat as it brushed against my face. I was happy to endure all of that just to get my hands on this new jet aircraft which a few short years ago had been in combat in WWII. My "wings" presented a few weeks ago were still shining new and a recognition of my ability which I was about to stretch today.

I adjusted the rudders fully back, not only to take any asymmetric loads more easily but, to get the knees bent to take more G before the greyout[20] turned to blackout. For the same reasons I put the seat fully down. The seat height could be adjusted from just seeing over the instrument panel to having your head touching the canopy, in latched increments. I was counting and timing the start cycle to get the cocks and levers in the right place as the engines wound up, from the plugged in trolley full of batteries with the airman standing beside it. Engines did not always start first time which made the thought of putting one out at low level, as was done for practice, a bit twitchy. Even if it did give longer range the relight in the air could be quite a performance.

As a qualified pilot, I felt that by doing the "vital actions", the pre-take-off checks, as I taxied to the take off runway it showed a certain air of professionalism. With Jet engines there was no need to test all the power and RPM range before take-off as was needed on a piston engine. I could then taxy straight onto the runway and take-off, all in one smooth action.

[19] A white gel used to style hair Fighter pilots were nickname "Brylcreem boys" by some of the papers.
[20] As G increased there was a period when the world became black and white then grey followed by gradual loss of sight as Blackout followed, if G was increased further, then loss of consciousness.

As I lined up I reached up to pull down the tinted goggles only to find that they were hanging down the back of my helmet. That caused some consternation as with my left hand firmly holding the throttles wide open the speed increased rapidly and the other hand was needed to apply brake initially to maintain direction. Instead of just pulling the goggles down with the right hand I let go of the throttles and pulled the goggles over into position with the left. Fortunately the engines kept on going with no change in the throttle position.

OFF TO MAKE AN IMPRESSION

Clearing the airfield and changing radio frequency I rapidly reached climbing speed and headed for the airfield I intended to visit. Up into the lower levels of the stratosphere – I would go for height to get the range I wanted. The little airfield had been disused since the war but the attraction was my girlfriend, Moira. She worked in the Air Ministry buildings still in use on the airfield and one of her colleagues, a wartime RAF pilot of Central European extraction, would be able to explain the excellence of the aerobatics that I had planned to show.

I could see both the east and west coasts as I closed the throttles and started a gentle descent. Not too fast or the Critical Mach Number[21] would be reached and then I would be out of control. As I got lower I increased the speed — if I could reach 500 knots I could get that lovely "blue note" as I came over the airfield. The Meteor produced a unique high pitched sound as it approached about 500 knots, which was the maximum permitted airspeed. I could now see the town some way from the airfield, fields and hills covered with pine forests, the runways and black hangars and the factory at the edge of the airfield.

I went past the factory chimney about half way up it and going flat out. There were forested hills in the distance and I wanted all the power on to climb out of trouble should I need it. I started a beautifully slow roll, not too much top rudder as I was going so fast but, in order to stay level, a firm push on the round top of the stick as I came inverted.

NOW THE UNEXPECTED

There was a thump as the top of my leather helmet hit the canopy, my feet were dangling off the rudder pedals and I could just reach the stick

---

[21] The speed when compressibility effects made the aircraft controls change both feel and effectiveness.

with my right hand but I could no longer apply bank. Dirt and dust from the floor had shot up into the canopy and managed to get under my goggles and into my eyes — but I must force them open.

When I had strapped in and put the seat fully down it had passed the bottom latch and now the negative G had shot the unlocked seat into the top of the cockpit. As I passed the Airfield Offices I was still flying level while inverted but the hills which had been in the distance were rapidly approaching with the ground rising to meet me. I could just aim for a big fire-break in the trees to give maximum thinking time. I kicked the stick into the far right corner of the cockpit with my foot; the negative G tweaked my neck and the Meteor flicked right way up. As the seat crashed back to the bottom of the cockpit I grabbed the stick and pulled back, just skirting the treetops beside the fire-break. That was rather too close for comfort and a sharp lesson, I was thinking as I climbed sedately back up.

As I climbed I found I was sweating but cold. I took off my oxygen mask and wiped my mouth with the back of my glove. As I did so I moved my head to look in the rear view mirror while my oxygen mask was dangling — I looked decidedly green. No worse than getting shot at, I supposed as I got down to the navigation back to base. Moira told me later that the Pilot beside her had said "Now, that's real flying!" So, I didn't frighten them too much — but That was close!

ANOTHER PROBLEM

Now, to find my way back to Base, those two fuel gauges looked a bit lower than I had expected at this stage of the flight. Perhaps it was going to be a bit tight on fuel. In that case I had better do the last bit, at low level, on one engine after all. The two fuel tanks were arranged so that the forward one fed the port engine and the aft the starboard engine. There was an interconnecting valve so that on the steep descent I intended to do I could open the valve and allow all the fuel to drain into the front tank. This meant the starboard engine would have to be shut down. The single engine landing was not difficult and I was well used to doing them. The electrics were run off the port engine so the radio would work OK. But, the hydraulics were worked by the starboard engine so I had to land at the first attempt or do an overshoot with the undercarriage and flaps dangling — hard work! With all the fuel in the tank for the port engine and the starboard one shut down I hoped that there was no trouble with my only engine as changing engines would be very tricky. At least I had not been up at high altitude for all of the flight. That could lead to all sorts of problems if the windscreen and instruments became so cold that they became covered in ice after a fast descent. Ice on the instruments sometimes had to be scratched off to see them and the canopy wound open to see the airfield. The most important instrument was the Airspeed indicator and often just scratching a small window of ice in the critical sector of the circular dial was enough to be safe on the approach. It was a classic return. A gentle join into the Circuit to go Downwind and "Finals on One", to let the Tower know one engine was shut down, touchdown beside the runway caravan and an easy turn-off. I counted the seconds and tickled the fuel cock down to relight the engine but then I realised it was not going to start. Difficult to explain the necessity to call for a tow after landing so I tried again. The second time the engine started and there was enough fuel to return to the dispersal — but That was close!

EXCITING ASYMMETRIC

Single engine landings had to be practiced regularly and on one occasion I was nearly "caught out" by getting low and slow on a single engine approach. I was at the end of the Downwind leg with gear and flap set and at the right speed to turn in with a curved approach to land. I was turning into the live engine as I had done many times before. As I came round the final turn I realised that I was a bit low and slow, and not yet pointing at the runway. I had misjudged the cross-wind, now blowing from behind me. I had my leg fully extended to give full rudder into the engine and so any increase in power was going to turn me away from the runway, and I didn't have enough fuel to go round for another attempt. Landing without enough fuel to make a second approach was quite common at that time and quite a few students ended up in a heap on the final approach. Having spent my time to get my "Wings" on twin engine Oxfords I was very familiar with the limitations and operation of a twin engine aircraft on one engine. This was a time to make innovative actions to get safely on the ground! I took all the power off the engine and the nose swung round under full rudder to face about 45 degrees into wind across the runway I then put on full power, the rate of descent stopped, and as I climbed back to join the correct descent path the nose swung around to align with runway. Gently easing off the power I was down on the runway and breathing rather hard.
That was a bit close!

Chapter 5

Meteor Mk 8

First flown 17th April 1952

FIGHTER PILOT

Having converted onto the Meteor Mk IV I was now off to the Fighter OCU[22] to fly the latest Meteor, the Mk 8. Fig.9. This was the latest RAF fighter with up-rated engines, improved flying controls, a different rudder configuration, a canopy operated by an electric motor and a Mk 1 Ejection Seat. Quite a step forward, but it was still armed with four 20mm Cannon firing forward from the nose of the aircraft and a WWII gyro gun-sight. We had to see and recognise the "wicked enemy", set the gun-sight for the enemy aircraft type and then track the target before firing. So, good eyesight was required and good aircraft recognition needed to be effective. In the cockpit the stick was not like the WWII round handled top of the MK IV but was a single "broom-handle" affair that I preferred. We were still using the aide memoire given to Fighter Pilots in WWII. Fig.35.

LIVE FIRING

We practiced using the gun-sight on other students in pairs of aircraft and fired live rounds on targets towed behind a piston engine aircraft of various types. Sometimes these targets were a flag and sometimes a drogue[23]. I preferred shooting at the drogue because you could see it rotate when you hit it. The flag was continually flapping so it was difficult to see that you had made a hit.

SQUADRON LIFE

Then I was off to my first Squadron. Many of the Squadron Pilots were very experienced and some had seen action in WWII and some skirmishes afterwards around the world. As a new boy it was difficult to fit immediately into the culture because so much was assumed without being briefed for a flight. The way in which we flew was a minimum of two aircraft "a pair", with the normal section of a "Battle Formation" of two pairs. We would take off and land as a pair, so close formation became second nature.

To get up above cloud the two pairs would take off at 10 second intervals and any turns in cloud would be followed by the second pair 10 seconds later. By doing this when we popped out of cloud we were all within sight of each other and could form up into Battle Formation, roughly pairs flying line abreast. This was known as a "Snake Climb". The joke briefing at the time was; "Follow me, SOP, last one off

---

[22] Operational Conversion Unit.
[23] A Drogue was like a large Windsock, of the sort used on airfields for wind direction and strength.

is number three, checks on the roll, we'll recover through a hole". That meant, I'm the leader for this trip, Standard Operating Procedures, we will do take off checks, known as "Vital actions", while taxiing for take-off, if number two is late number three will slot into his place, we'll try not to get into cloud on our return to base!

FIRST AIRCRAFT LOSS

I was in close formation as Number 2 in the second pair on such a Snake Climb in fairly dense cloud. To my surprise I saw a Meteor 8 passing vertically down with the tail missing. The No.2 in the first pair had knocked off the tail of the leader, and it was the leader of the formation I saw going down.

Initially we thought; "that's another one gone!" But, this was a very early use of the Mk1 Ejection Seat and the Leader parachuted to safety, if a little shaken by the experience.

There was very little automation on the first ejection seats. The safety harness that fitted over the parachute harness was attached to the seat instead of to the aircraft. The canopy had to be manually jettisoned before firing the seat, and once out of the aircraft the safety harness was then released to fall free of the seat. Then the parachute was operated manually, just as was done when you just jumped over the side to escape from the aircraft. The training was to be shot up a ramp in an ejection seat using about a half charge in the explosive motor. This gave you some idea of the kick in the seat of the pants to expect.

During the time of my training and operating Meteors there was a very high rate of fatal accidents. Before ejection seats were fitted, at times, there would be as many as several fatalities in a week. The newspapers of the day reported some of them but we became used to seeing holes in the ground all around the Meteor training airfields. You may think this is an exaggeration because the RAF training accidents records for Meteors in the 1950s seem to have long gone. However, those who lived through it will confirm what I say, probably with a sharp intake of breath.

At about this time another peculiar set of accidents happened. The Rubber Dinghy which we sat on in the ejection seat was inadvertently inflating in the cockpit! There was no escape, the protruding Dinghy pushed the stick forward and the aircraft crashed out of control. Having identified the problem we were all fitted out with a knife sewn on the leg of our flying suit so that if this happened we could cut a hole in the Dinghy and prevent it inflating dangerously.

MASS FORMATION

The other interesting event I remember from that era was being on a "Balbo", a very large formation was known after the Italian General renowned for amassing large gaggles of aircraft in the same bit of sky. Fig.6. We had been out across France in Battle Formation but then the Squadron closed up into close formation– "Pansy Formation" as it was known. The Boss decided he would show off his chaps to another airfield so we thundered across it only to find another lot of Pansies overflying. It turned out to be a flypast for the Inspection of the Air Officer Commanding so I think our Boss had more than a red face when we got back to Base.

DOG FIGHTING

It was not unusual to be "jumped" by aircraft of another Country when over the coast or the Channel because there were European and American aircraft in great numbers. I got mixed up with a huge practice dogfight over the Channel on one occasion. There were Sabres and Venoms up at the top Meteors, Vampires, and American Thunderjets in the middle and French P47s down at the bottom. The pundits who said that the advent of jets would end the era of dogfighting were so wrong, as was proved in Korea and the Vietnam War. Fighter aircraft had much open airspace in those days. There were very few airways, and they only extended up to 10,000 feet. Airliners and bombers were piston engine and did not operate at the heights of the fighters. Also the public were used to seeing military aircraft flashing around the countryside amongst the trees from their wartime experience so no eyebrows were raised if it happened.

EARLY SCIENTIFIC JUDGEMENTS

This new era of aviation led to a number of poor pieces of advice being given to the UK Government of the day by Scientific Advisers. One was that the human reflexes needed to fly jet fighters had to be so sharp that after the age of about 26 fighter pilots would no longer be able to cope, because of the deterioration of reflex action with age! Another was that Man could not live at Supersonic Speed so there was no point in pursuing the design of aircraft capable of flying at supersonic speeds. The Miles Aircraft Company was in the process of designing just such an aircraft. The project was scrapped and as we were sharing scientific knowledge with our American Allies at the time the design somehow passed to them. The American Bell X–1 which was the first aircraft to fly at supersonic speed looked very much like the design of the Miles M52 – even the critical bit of design of the "all-flying" tailplane. This tailplane moved as a whole and no longer relied upon elevators at the end of the control surface, thus providing the tail forces to balance the shift in the lift forces caused by supersonic flight.

A DIFFERENCE OF OPINION

One of the strange things about some of the briefings was that some facets were not mentioned because they were part of the culture. As a "new boy" I found I was sometimes not sure what was required of me. As an example I was preparing for a night sortie and because I was the "New Boy" I was last to get the navigation equipment to plan the flight. While I had still not finished planning, the Boss came in and wanted to know why I wasn't airborne and chased me off into the air. As a result I got a bit lost and had to get homing bearings from ATC to get back to Base.

Another problem was, on a large formation sortie I was briefed as No.4 to be "In the Box", flying line astern to the leader. My instructions were clear, "Keep the leader in the top of the windscreen arch". I later discovered I had been flying out of position because it was the leader's engines which should have been in the top of the arch, not his wing-tips! So, I was well out of position and was accused of being frightened to stay close. I was also a bit wild with my flying when not in a pair and just practicing the handling of the aircraft. The upshot was that my Tour of Duty was cut short and I was sent off to fly Varsities.

Chapter 6

Varsity

First flown 27th November 1952

LIFE AS A "STAFF PILOT" AT A NAVIGATION SCHOOL

I first met the Varsity Figs.10 and 12. when I went to an Operational Conversion Unit in preparation to become a Staff Pilot, training Student Navigators at an Air Navigation Training School. At the O.C.U there were two aircraft types; rather tired Wellington Bombers, left over from WWII, and the shining new Varsities. Looking back it would have been nice to have had the experience of flying a Wellington but at the time I was glad to be selected to convert to the Varsity.

The Varsity was the first specially designed aircraft to train Pilots, Navigators and Bomb Aimers for the RAF after WWII. In the cockpit was a place for two Pilots, each with complete flight instruments; while behind the cockpit was a place for a Signaller and behind him two navigation tables, set side by side, for Navigators. With two monstrous double-banked 18 cylinder air cooled radial engines the Varsity was a good example of a twin piston engine trainer of the era. On one engine it could out-perform some of the single engine trainers still in RAF use at the time. It had the range to fly from the UK to the Mediterranean and would cruise at 10.000 feet with the two stage superchargers running.

I came to enjoy flying it and training the Navigators, even though there was not a working autopilot at the time. Most of the other Staff Pilots were veterans of WWII bombers, flying deep into the heart of Germany and back, for hours without an autopilot so I took this as the natural state of affairs. This was my introduction to aircraft new to the RAF that, unfortunately, did not work as designed for some time after they were in service.

THE TASK

The job of Staff Pilot was to fly the aircraft on the Courses and to ETA's (Estimated Time of Arrival) set by the Student Navigators in the aircraft. As students they were quite likely to make errors in navigation, but it was the pilot's duty to follow what the student wanted. However, as Aircraft Captain the Staff Pilot had to himself navigate to know exactly where the aircraft was, and was going, at all times. Also, as Captain I was charged with the overall safety of the flight; not to stray into restricted airspace, to ensure a safe altitude was maintained and there was enough fuel remaining to return to Base and any Alternate Airfield.

Flights with the students consisted of several legs around the UK ending back at base. One pilot would fly if there was a trip of about four hours and a second pilot would come along if the sorties were more like eight hours.

Being a Staff Pilot was quite a challenge at times when a student read the heading required for the next leg from the wrong column on his log and then asked me to fly the direction of the Indicated Airspeed! Or they just got the sums wrong and turned early or late on a leg. I would always have my own log and flight plan on my knee pad and kept a meticulous record of what was actually happening.

As well as the Students on-board we carried a Signaller. He would keep in communication with Headquarters by Wireless Transmission and send position reports to Air Traffic Control Centres. Most Signallers also had charts for a radio aid called Consul which used intersecting radio signals to give a position on the chart. Sometimes the Signallers would become quite agitated when they saw that the Students were straying too far from the assigned track. I always let the Students stray as far as I dared to let them learn from their errors. These became apparent at the debriefing by Navigation Instructors who were charged with teaching them. That was part of their training sortie that I was spared.

After a while I could find my way very accurately around the UK by day or night, and in all sorts of weather. The Varsity had a good de-icing system on the wings and propellers so blundering around in thick cloud, with ice flying off the props and whacking the fuselage, was not something to worry about. We would be in contact with other aircraft from the Base on the same route and would pass back information on icing, turbulence and cloud conditions. Sometimes this helped to change altitude to get a smoother ride. When map reading was not available I had to rely on radio beacons and bearings on the VHF[24] radio from Military Airfields to calculate my position, and that was an art form in itself.

I did have one crew who instead of turning over a Scottish Coastal town to go south started off for Norway. Soon a very agitated Signaller appeared in the cockpit pointing at his Consul chart in incredulity. I reassured him that I knew what was going on and would turn while we still had plenty of fuel to get back to Base. We did just that.

---

[24] Very High Frequency radio, short range, used for radio telephony.

MORE EXCITING MOMENTS

I did have some exciting events while flying the Varsity. On two occasions I found that the Pitot/Static[25] system had failed so I had to really fly "by the seat of my pants". The pressure driven Flight Instruments were showing wildly conflicting indications between the two "Blind Flying[26]" panels for the two pilot positions in the cockpit; pilot's seats were side by side. None of these instruments seemed to be correct, on either panel. So, only the Artificial Horizon, which was by now electrically driven, Compass, and the Engine Instruments were showing correct information. I had lost the Airspeed, Altimeter, and Rate of Climb and Descent Instruments, all pretty essential to fly the aircraft safely. When you have been taught from the beginning of your Instrument Flying not to rely on any sensations but to always believe your instruments, it takes a moment or two to "get your head round" what is going on and analyse how to deal with the situation. The first occasion was in visual conditions. I knew the power settings and attitude the aircraft had to have to fly around a circuit and make an approach and landing, so I told the Tower, just in case it all went wrong, and flew around for a safe landing. A bit scary and probably not the best landing that I ever did in the Varsity.

AND AGAIN

The same problem happened again while on Detachment to Germany. Towards the end of their Course the Navigation Students were taken overseas. Sometimes into German bases and often down to the Mediterranean, to Gibraltar or Tripoli in Libya. This time I was in cloud and climbing before I discovered the problem. The aircraft popped out the top of the cloud and got stabilised in the cruise and called the Tower. Fortunately one of our own Varsities, on the Detachment, was in the locality so we met up and I did a formation let-down and landing through the cloud with him leading.

It was discovered that the Ground Crew on climbing into the nosewheel bay, to get at equipment behind the instrument panels to mend it, had stood on the Pitot/Static pipes running along the side of the undercarriage bay and distorted their shape. Sometimes some of the pipes were squashed flat so there was virtually no air getting through. No wonder the instrument indications were showing such discrepancies!

---

[25] The pipes that carry the outside atmospheric pressure and the pressure from the speed of the aircraft through the air to instruments showing things like airspeed and altitude.
[26] The panels in front of the pilots holding the instruments showing aircraft performance so the pilot can fly in cloud. See Glossary for more.

THE VARSITY AS A GLIDER

The Varsity had a Vacuum Pump on each engine. Each Instrument Panel had instruments using gyros driven by suction and in particular a large Reid and Sigrist Turn and Bank indicator. That instrument went back to early flying in cloud even before the Artificial Horizon had been invented. There were air filters on the suction driven instruments and these sometimes affected the airflow and hence the accuracy of the gyros. There was a problem with the instruments on this aircraft and it was identified as the Vacuum Pumps misbehaving, but could not be fully checked on the ground. So, the Engineering Officer and I took the aircraft up on a day of clear blue sky to check the pumps.

There was a plan to fly at about 1000 feet over the sea, so that there would be maximum atmospheric pressure to help the Vacuum Pump operation, and shut down each engine in turn.

I was looking forward to the opportunity to shut down engines because you seldom got a chance to practice "Feathering" an engine and this was a chance to practice the drills and hone the skills. Shutting down the engine involved reducing the RPM and setting the propeller end on to the airflow, feathering, before shutting off Ignition and Fuel. I shut down the first engine and the Engineer Officer took his readings I started up that engine and then Feathered the second engine for him to make his measurements of that Vacuum Pump.

This went on for several times, shutting and starting engines, and I was becoming adept at the Drills for Engine Shut-down and could do them very rapidly. The Engineer Officer was having some trouble getting the readings he wanted and said "OK Next" and I immediately, and foolishly, stopped the running engine! We were now over the sea at 1000 feet with no engines running! Should I try to restart one of the engines, which one? Should I try for starting both and see how many started? I chose to restart both engines at once and my hands flashed over the cocks and controls, leaving the Varsity to glide gently towards the sea. Both engines roared into life and I climbed back up to 1000 feet. The Engineer Officer decided that he had enough information, on this particular problem, so we returned to Base and decamped to the bar.

That was a bit close!

EVEN MORE EXCITING

Before I leave the Varsity there was one other occasion when I had rather an exciting time. I was due to take some students on a night flying navigation exercise. The Commanding Officer of the Anson aircraft that were also operating at the Base was interested in the shiny new Varsities and asked to come along with me as a Second Pilot. It was not a trip that was long enough for another pilot to be used, and anyway he was not qualified to operate a Varsity. He just "came along for the ride" and to wonder at the difference in performance of the Varsity over the Anson. He was impressed with the Take off performance and the rate of climb and soon we were settled at cruising height with the Students sweating away with their sums down the back at their navigation tables.

Between the pilots and the student navigators was the Signallers Position. He had a radio setup that allowed him to communicate by HF and operate the IFF[27], equivalent to today's Transponder[28] now used by Civil Aircraft but then only used by Military Aircraft.
The pilots used the VHF radio housed beside the HF Equipment and generally talked to Air Traffic Control while the Signaller passed Position Reports on HF to Headquarters and ATC Centres.
It was a clear night with a good horizon and many shining stars and I was telling the Anson CO how to fly straight when looking out ahead.

It was the custom to settle for a star up in a corner of the windscreen and fly to that rather than constantly having your head inside the cockpit looking at the instruments. Suddenly the curtains behind us, used to keep the cockpit dark, were thrust aside by the Signaller. Behind him was a blaze of light and smoke billowed past him from the rear of the aircraft into the cockpit. He had removed his helmet and so shouted above the roar of the engines, "The radio's on fire!"

Now, there had been many discussions in the Crew Room about situations where the Captain needs to get information about what is happening in the bowels of the aircraft in an emergency: does the Captain leave the controls to another pilot or does he send the Second Pilot back to report the situation. Well, I didn't have a qualified Second Pilot, although I was sure the CO of Anson's could have flown straight and level while I left the controls, so I said to him "Go and see what is happening". To the Signaller I said" Put on the Asbestos Gloves, unbolt the radio and if it is still burning cut a hole in the aircraft with the fire axe and throw it out!"

[27] A device that sent back a coded signal to ground based radar for aircraft identification.
[28] Similar device to IFF now used for all aircraft in Controlled Airspace.

At that time all large RAF aircraft carried as part of the Emergency Kit large gauntlet gloves made of asbestos and a firemen's axe. You might think that a bit drastic but only a few years before such actions were being done by crews on aircraft crippled by enemy action.

The Anson CO had taken off his helmet when leaving his seat so now both he and the Signaller were off Intercom so I was not sure what was happening between me and my Students. Just behind the radios the main spar, which held the wings on, ran across the fuselage. You had to climb over it when passing through the aircraft, and I feared that if the fire was spreading in might cause that to fail and we would all be in the drink. We were flying over the Irish Sea while this was going on.

So, I gave the order "Put on Parachutes". Seeing the Students donning their parachutes the Anson's CO appeared back in the cockpit to put his parachute on. I got him to put on his helmet and tell me what was happening. The VHF Radio had caught fire but was now extinguished but useless and the fire had not spread.

While all this commotion was going on it had taken my attention from the engine instruments. We had automatic gills on the Engine Oil Coolers but the AUTO setting did not work at this time. These, together with the Autopilot, had not worked since the introduction of the Varsity. We pilots learned to "live with" these deficiencies, as pilots have lived with deficiencies forever. This meant that periodically the Gills had to be adjusted manually. I had failed to pay attention to this and I now had one engine very badly overheating and about to catch fire. I had no option but to shut down that engine. Now I was on one engine with fire damage and no VHF Radio. Still, we could now take off the parachutes and settle down while I took us back to base, while informing Headquarters and the ATC Centre on HF what was going on.

ANOTHER SURPRISE WAS WAITING

That was enough for one night, I was thinking, as we approached Base. However, there another surprise was waiting, Base was shut due to dense fog and most of the rest of the country was rapidly approaching similar conditions. Having over-flown Base and circled we could now only communicate by Aldis Lamp, like a large flashlight with a trigger to flash Morse Code[29].

---

[29] A set of short and long transmissions, sound or light, representing letters of the alphabet.

The poor Signaller had not had to read flashing Morse Code for years so it took a bit of time before we got the message fully. I was to divert to the North of Scotland where there were airfields still open.

I set course for Scotland and the Signaller got on the HF to get the latest weather information. Shortly after I had set course the Signaller called me to say that an airfield that we would pass by in a few minutes was just going out in fog but they would put all the runway and approach lights on full brightness and they had Sodium Lighting.

This was before Mr. Calvert of Royal Aircraft Establishment at Farnborough had invented the "Centreline and Crossbar" lighting. That had a line of lights extending back up the approach from the runway. Across these at intervals were crossbars of lights, to give horizontal orientation. The clever thing was that these bars got smaller as you approached the runway and if you were at the correct height to pass over them they seemed to be the same length – reassuring you that you were on the correct descent path to the runway. Fig.27.

Alas, my problem was that at the time WWII lighting still prevailed at RAF airfields and was considered to be adequate. Fig.29.
It was worth a try, landing in poor visibility was something I had practiced many times previously and these new Sodium Lights, like today's orange coloured street-lights, were very bright. What I was not sure of was, are these particular lights along the runway or down the approach. However, there was not time to have long discussions by HF when the visibility was getting worse all the time.

The other thing on my mind was the engine I had shut down. I was sure that I had caught the overheating before much damage had been done, so I could restart it as the Oil Cooler would now be able to be monitored and set correctly. Restarting a shut down engine is not something to be considered lightly. I could not talk to ATC at this airfield as I made my approach to land so, if I had to manoeuvre at low level because I arrived unexpectedly, it would be better to be flying on two engines. So, I restarted the "dead" engine and prepared to try to land at the airfield going out in fog. To let them know I was coming I put on the Landing Lights. This is something we did not normally use, especially in fog, but at least the ATC in the Tower would see where we ended up! I found the runway and landed with plenty of room to spare. We left the aircraft for the Ground Crew to put to bed and headed for the bar. But, That was close!

If that sort of series of events took place today I shudder to think how many pages of report and inquiry would be involved. I recall no paperwork at all being done except the Aircraft Technical Log to mend the broken bits. All of my Colleagues and Superiors were ex-WWII people who had seen action and aircraft returning with bits hanging off as part of routine returns to Base. They were just going to accept such events as not unusual and we all got on with the job in hand. The Anson's Boss never flew with me in a Varsity again. However, he did let me fly one of his Anson's, and that made me realise what an ancient aircraft they were. I was glad it was a Varsity I was flying on that Tour of Duty.

COMMENDATION

When I ended that Tour, flying the Varsity, the Base closed. I subsequently found I had been awarded the King's Commendation for Valuable Service in the Air. By the time it was promulgated I was on a Jet Refresher Course and Her Majesty Queen Elizabeth was enthroned so it became the Queen's Commendation!

Chapter 7

Meteors again

ANOTHER CHANCE TO FLY A METEOR

After flying so many hours on an aircraft using piston engines as a Staff Pilot I was sent off to do a "Jet Refresher" Course. This was to refresh the skills used to operate at high speeds and high altitudes with rather temperamental jet engines. I was delighted to find that I was to fly again the Mark 8 Meteor, the same Mark that I had flown on a Fighter Squadron. I was even more delighted to find that my Instructor was to be a chap who was a few years ahead of me at the same school! We had a great rapport and he soon found there was not much he could teach me about the Meteor. We also enjoyed doing formation aerobatics together.

AN EARLY LESSON IN HUMAN ERROR

I was thoroughly at home in the Meteor and enjoyed flying with the Flight Commander for a check ride. I had found that in two seat jets I could often pull so much G without blacking out that the other occupant would be blacked out well before me. This Flight Commander was of "sterner stuff" and we each did our aerobatic performance to the acclaim of the other.
The aircraft began to descend in a gradual turn, so I said "Are we going low flying now?" to which he said "I thought you were flying it!" We quickly sorted out who was flying and returned to Base more quietly!
That was a bit close!

A CHANGE OF OPINION

Remarkably, I left the Course with assessments of all aspects assessed as Above the Average, except Formation for which I was given Exceptional So, there did seem to be a difference of opinion about my flying ability, between Fighter Command and Training Command. My flying was never again called into question and I was "at the sharp end" of the RAF, flying each new aircraft in the role, from then on! So, on to the next Tour of Operations – Night Fighters in Germany. The generous financial allowances given to personnel in Germany prompted me to marry Moira and we were set to have a good start to our new life together.

Chapter 8

Canberra

First flown 24th November 1954

BOMBER COMMAND!

It was a bit of a surprise to find myself about to fly a Canberra Fig.11. and to become part of Bomber Command. Having just completed a Jet Refresher course flying Meteor Mk8 aircraft and impressed the Staff so that they recommended my posting to Night Fighters in Germany, Bomber Command had not been mentioned. But, such is life in the Armed Forces – you can never be sure where you will be sent and what you might be asked to do.

The Canberra was the first jet bomber for the RAF. It replaced the Lincoln, which was like a WWII Lancaster made a bit bigger and better, powered by four piston engines. As a jet bomber the Canberra was to last for many years in a variety of roles because it performed so well. Although not particularly fast it could operate at altitudes well above most other aircraft of the time of its inception. The single pilot sat in a cockpit covered by a dome shaped canopy with a navigator and bomb-aimer sat behind and all had ejection seats. The first quirky thing the pilot noticed was that the instrument panel was, for some unknown reason, not in the standard RAF presentation. Fig.20

Also the Climb and Descent meter worked "back to front" on initiating a turn. It showed Climb if descending and Descent if climbing and took a while to get used to when trying to maintain an accurate height turning onto a bombing run!

For some time the Canberra provided some interesting problems. The moveable tail plane had a habit of occasionally running away to full trim either full nose up or full nose down. If the aircraft was at medium altitude and going at normal cruising speed this made it almost impossible to recover the aircraft. Part of the solution was to limit the extent of travel, and hence amount of trim, on the movement of the tail-plane. Because of the high probability of this runaway it was decided to have Pilots practice flying the aircraft with full nose down trim. Just to make it more exciting there was a requirement for Pilots to demonstrate the ability to perform an instrument flying missed approach, flying on one engine, on limited panel instruments (no Artificial Horizon) with the trim full nose down, landing gear down and full flap extended!

OUT OF BREATH…

The Canberra handled very well and although I was content to perform the odd Barrel Roll I was never brave enough to perform a loop. However, after I had left the Canberra behind, the pilots who were taught how to deliver a Tactical Nuclear Weapon released it as they started a loop. Then when over the top and starting down they rolled over and pulled out at ground level and off, away from the ensuing blast!

One of the exciting times I had we extricated ourselves from with the help of my Navigator. The Canberra was well pressurised and because we could fly at great altitude we had to wear Pressure Breathing Waistcoats and Pressure Breathing Oxygen Masks. This gave the capability to breathe without pressurisation at high altitude, say 50,000 feet, and still function operationally. The Oxygen Mask was not attached to the main supply but was fed from the connection on the Pressure Waistcoat. One night as we were climbing up to cruising altitude my Navigators became concerned about my behaviour and demeanour. I insisted that they get on with the job and stop wittering. However, the Navigator appeared at my right shoulder, having bravely unstrapped and come forward saying: "You should check your oxygen"! He was right, my oxygen mask tube had somehow detached from the Waistcoat and I was breathing just cockpit air. The symptoms of lack of oxygen are rather like early stages of inebriation and the flesh under the finger nails and around the lips shows a blue tinge. As soon as the Mask was attached again to the Waistcoat and I was on oxygen I realised what was going on and we returned to Base for me to do a medical check. An early lesson for me in good Crew Coordination.

HOW MANY WHEELS?

I did have another rather exciting event when I had undercarriage problems. At that time it was not unusual for aircraft to be taken away for a weekend by flying a Navigation Exercise to some Base conveniently close to some Loved One or Party. A Chap from the Operations Room at our Base wanted to go off for the weekend so My Navigator and I volunteered to drop him off at the airfield of his choice and then immediately fly back. There was a "Jump Seat" that could be set across the access to the rear crew position and he sat there. The only problem with that was that he had to wear a parachute harness but that was worth the effort to hitch a ride.

We joined the circuit at the airfield and I did the Landing Checks, only to find that there was no nose-wheel green light! I tried all manner of manoeuvres to get a green light, wheels up and down, pitch up and down, side-slip and "G" forces. It soon became clear that this was going to be a bit of an "arrival" with no nose-wheel. I decided that a return to Base was in order. As we had plenty of fuel to go back at low level I would alert Base to the problem, so they could make preparations, but would continue to shake the aircraft about while on the way. The question I was considering was: will Base want me to land on a foam strip on the runway or on the grass beside the runway? The shaking worked and at last we had the three green lights – undercarriage securely down. I went straight in and landed very gently, then left the aircraft to the Ground Crew.

I thought nothing of it really except it was a bit exciting, until I returned to work. The Ground Crew had an astounding story to tell. The problem had not been in the hydraulic actuator that moved the wheel up and down. The attachment of the end of the actuator to the fuselage bulkhead had sheared. By manoeuvring I had managed to lock the broken end of the actuator under the attachment on the bulkhead and the air pressure from the aircraft speed kept it in place. Once on the ground the weight of the aircraft kept the actuator in place and so the landing and taxiing was accomplished with a very precarious situation. I was glad it was a gentle landing and my "luck was in" on the day, but it was close, and the poor passenger missed his weekend away.

Another little foible with the Canberra B2 was due to the construction and shape of the cockpit canopy. On a dark night, and in rain, during an instrument approach if you suddenly saw the runway lights quite late there was an illusion of two sets of runway lights. This happened when landing in rain giving poor visibility and if the wrong set of runway lights was chosen it resulted in a low approach. Sometimes so low that you could end up landing short of the runway, or even in the last of the approach lights! Best not to aim for the near end of the runway but to stay on the rate of descent from the PAR[30] Controller and accept a landing well along the runway at the Radar touchdown point.

A friend of mine who had been flying Varsities at the same Base that I flew from converted to the Canberra at the same time as me. He had this double set of lights appear on final approach. Realising he was aiming too low he applied full power – too late, he hit the approach lights. As full power took effect the debris went into one engine and it failed. This sudden change in power and attitude left him upside down over the start of the runway at low level! No chance for them to eject at that height, and upside down. So he calmly, but somewhat excitedly, took all the power off, rolled the aircraft upright and landed on what was left of the runway. I recall this was on a Friday night and I was off Base visiting my wife in our

---

[30] Precision Approach Radar The Controller gave the pilot corrections in direction and descent to make an accurate approach to the runway.

rented rooms for the weekend. By the time I returned on Monday he had decided to resign from the RAF and give up flying. He could not be persuaded that his saving of the aircraft was a remarkable feat of airmanship. He went off to civil life but the urge to earn a crust by flying was still there. I met him later when he was a Check Captain on a major airline. He beat me into civil flying by several years.

A GRAND PLAN

Main Force, Bomber Command was not a very exciting role with the most exciting bit being that the Squadron moved to a new Base shortly after I joined. However, it soon became clear that the "Authorities" had a Grand Plan for me which was why I had come to Bomber Command. I fitted the profile of experience and ability to be sent on the new V-Force that was to be formed. I was sent to convert to Valiant Bombers.

NOT FOR THE FAINT HEARTED

My wife, Poor Moira, who had accepted my proposal of marriage thinking of a life of comparative luxury in Germany had a shock. She was now faced with me going from aircraft conversion course to aircraft conversion course and a series of rented accommodation places, not for the faint hearted! She supported me nobly and helped with my learning – she could give a very good lecture on the operation of the autopilot!

Chapter 9

THE FIRST 4 JET V-BOMBER

Valiant B1

First flown 7th February 1956

The Valiant Fig.13. was the first of the Nuclear Deterrent force, the V-Force, aircraft of the RAF. There were to be the Valiant, Vulcan and Victor aircraft in the role. This was the force designed to give the UK a significant advantage at the start of what was to become known as the Cold War. It was a swept wing, four jet, high altitude, high speed bomber designed to carry the UK Atom Bomb. It carried Captain, Co-pilot, Navigator, Bomb-aimer and a Signaller[31] who was charged with Long Range Communications and Electronic Countermeasures. Our Signaller was fluent in Russian and that was useful when we got close to the Iron Curtain and could hear fighters looking for us!

As a less experienced Bomber Pilot I was the Co-pilot in my crew. I was on an early course and on the first wing of squadrons and at that time we were all very enthusiastic. Most of the crews were very experienced Bomber People and they were now to operate in a whole new environment, faster, higher and with astonishingly devastating weapons. On most RAF courses the pass mark was maybe 80 to 85% for subjects but on this course there was so much enthusiasm that marks of 99 and 100% were commonplace. It was a nice atmosphere for the crew to begin to mould together.

The Valiant was a new type of aircraft trying an "all electric" philosophy. Almost all the actuators were electric motors, huge electric motors for the retraction of the undercarriage. This philosophy provided us with some problems at first and at one early stage all the aircraft were "grounded" while some electrical problems were diagnosed and fixed. This was the first of many groundings on new types of aircraft I was to fly in the RAF. However, the Valiant was a joy to fly because it handled well, manoeuvred well at high altitude and was easy to trim and set power on the approach and landing. Just what you needed after a long and arduous flight. The swept wing was a novelty to Bomber Crews and because a lot of the fuel was in wing tanks the Centre of Gravity of the aircraft had to be monitored when they were in use. That was the responsibility of the Co-pilot, so I became very adept with fuel booster pumps and a slide rule!

Another innovation was a doppler radar kit that showed the Track, the exact path over the ground, and the Ground-speed very accurately. Well, it didn't have a read-out of Track over the Ground but it showed very accurately the Drift Angle, the angle between the Aircraft Heading and the Track over the Ground. Thus as the Navigator knew the aircraft Heading,

---

[31] The more grand title of Air Electronics Officer was not yet invented.

from the compass, it only required minor mental gymnastics to work out the Track over the ground. This was a great leap forward in navigational accuracy. Previously both Track and Ground-speed had to be calculated from position observations derived from visual, radar or star shots, and timed between these successive positions. Although the Track direction could also be observed on radar this new kit was a huge improvement in accuracy.

Flying was now becoming much more "technical", or even scientific, in our operating methods. Attention was being paid to the limits of the Flight Envelope; the edges of operating limits of height, speed, engine performance and G forces. For example; suddenly there appeared a painted white line across the runway set at a distance from the start of the take-off run. This was to be the "Acceleration Check Point" which must be crossed at a minimum speed or take-off should be abandoned. This was not what Commercial Pilots know as the V_1 Speed, at which you can take-off or stop on the runway in the event of an emergency on the take-off run. Those eventualities were taken care of by two different speeds, a "V Go" speed and a "V Stop" which meant what they said. At Go you had enough runway left to take-off and at Stop you had enough runway to stop before you went off the end. Usually Go came before Stop, but when it was the other way round a couple of anxious moments ensued! This was all very strange to Bomber Pilots who were used to just "feeling the aircraft off the ground" and hopefully before the hedge at the end of the airfield.

A DIFFERENT ROLE

Having been all geared up for being a "Nuclear Force" we suddenly found we were practicing for a WWII type of operation. A Bomber Stream, aircraft arriving at the target in a long line, with targets marked by a Pathfinder[32], Target Indicator[33] and a Master Bomber[34] laying down more Coloured Target Markers[35] for us to drop visual sighted conventional bombs. Some of the Captains had seen it all before so we soon became proficient.

[32] In WWII the Pathfinder Force were a set of elite crews sent ahead of the Bomber Stream to identify the target.
[33] A flare on the ground indicating the general area of the target.
[34] A senior pilot flying in the target area and amending the aiming points for the Bomber Stream.
[35] Differed from Target Indicators because they were more specific aiming points.

While all this was going on we suddenly came to a heightened State of Readiness and armed for the Nuclear Role. There was an insurrection going on in Hungary and the politicians were not sure how the Iron Curtain[36] Countries were going to react. We often found that the political situation was more clear to us by our State of Readiness than what was being said publicly. Once, that crisis passed and we were again rigged for the conventional weapons, 1000lb bombs.

Shortly after that we were dispersed to a Mediterranean Island, with Valiants parked around in almost every available space. For some days we flew some practice bombing sorties and then were all called to a big briefing. "Gentlemen we are at War" was the opening phrase used by the Briefing Officer, our Station Commander. "The Egyptians have taken over the Suez Canal, the Israeli and Egyptian Forces are engaged and we are to attack Egypt." We were to attack airfield targets using the WWII tactics we had been practicing. There was much talk of what Night Fighters might be encountered and how high the Heavy Flak Batteries[37] could reach. Escape and Evasion procedures were briefed, packs of gold sovereigns and handguns were issued and I started to do some sums.

TIME TO GET THE SUMS RIGHT!

As Co-pilot I was charged with making the calculations of the aircraft performance for the take-off. The sums were all about whether a Valiant with a full bomb load could get airborne from the runway length available and in the weather conditions expected. If the wind and temperature were right we could just get off the ground before we ran out of runway!

There was much nervous tension amongst the crews – it was "Earn your money Time"! Many of the crews were veterans of WWII and had been through this before but some of the younger ones had some misgivings. For my part I felt that this was the culmination of my training and was eager to get on with the task. The Valiant with a full bomb load was a bit more sluggish than the usual jaunty handling and the take-off was going to be interesting. We were slow to accelerate but seemed to be gathering speed OK as the runway lights flashed past into the night. But then the end of the lights was rapidly approaching and we were still on the ground. At last, as we ran out of lights the Valiant lifted into the air –
but That was close!

---

[36] Countries in the Eastern Block of Communist Alliance.
[37] Groups of high powered anti-aircraft artillery
See Glossary.

REAL ACTION

The devious route the Bomber Stream took went smoothly. Our target was an airfield complex. We were not at the head of the Stream so we saw the Green Pathfinder Target Indicator go down and then the Red Target Marker from the Master Bomber. He was the chap who flew around the target and gave instructions on the amount of offset for the Bomb-aimers to use. There was a lot of Light Flak hosing about at low level but none of the heavy Flak in a Barrage[38] that we expected. Only occasional bits of Heavy Flack up near our altitude. Our young Bomb-aimer became rather over-excited as we ran in so I doubt if our bombs really were exactly on target. But, all our aircraft returned to Base so that was a good first effort.

FIRST RADAR BOMBS WITH NBS

Our second target was a Naval Installation and again the Bomber Stream trundled around a devious route before approaching the target. This time it was decided we would bomb using Radar. The Navigation and Bombing System (NBS) was a sort of hybrid system of WWII bomb-sight calculators and some new computing components. However, inside the boxes it still relied on mechanical shaped cams, mechanical relays and three dimensional surfaces over which a needle ran. I thought it rather like the fantastic imaginary machines that used to be drawn by the cartoonist Heath Robinson, but it was the best we had at the time. Certainly it was able to get an Atom Bomb close enough to the target. The radar part needed a good understanding of radar basic principles to be able to interpret the returns accurately. You had to know how the fuzzy blips on the screen were generated to know where the object generating the return was hiding. The original set of this type of radar, when it was invented in WWII, was thought to be so bad that someone remarked, "It stinks" – so it became known as H_2S. These were the chemical symbols for the gas Hydrogen Sulphide, which does indeed stink – it smells like rotten eggs!

The run in to the target was uneventful and we could see the Target Indicators on the ground showing the aiming point. But, partly because of the over-excitement from the young Bomb-aimer on our first attack, the Captain decided to use the Radar Bomb-aimer to release our bombs. Again we felt the aircraft lift as the bombs released, bomb doors closed and on the way back to base. At neither of the debriefings on our return could we say if we had really hit the target. Only the Master Bomber who was down low in

[38] A set of bursting shells from anti-aircraft artillery spread over the target at the height they expected the Bomber Stream.

Fig. 1. The Chipmunk was first RAF trainer aircraft to have a closed cockpit for the pilots.
Image: Tony Hisgett

Fig. 2. Piston Provost.
Image: Neil Lanwarne

Fig. 3. The Link Trainer was the 1930s equivalent of today's Flight Simulator. With the hood closed a pilot used the flight instruments to fly a three dimensional pattern or even a cross country route.
Image: Bzuk

Fig. 4. The author in 1951 with "Wings".
Note that in the tradition of a RAF fighter pilot my top button in undone.
Image: Author's own

Fig. 5. The author beside an Oxford at the time he was training for his "Wings".
Image: Author's own

Fig. 6. Meteor Mk 8s lined up before a stream take off in pairs for a "Balbo".
Image: Author's own

Fig. 7. Meteor Mk 4.
Image: RuthAS

Fig. 8. Meteor Mk 7.
The two seat trainer used to convert pilots to Meteor jet aircraft.
Image: MikeH

Fig. 9. Meteor Mk 8.
Image: Mike Freer

Fig. 10. Varsity training aircraft.
Image: Author's own

Fig. 11. The Canberra was the first jet bomber in the RAF.
Image: JohnnyOneSpeed

Fig. 12. The author in the Varsity formatting on another.
Image: Author's own

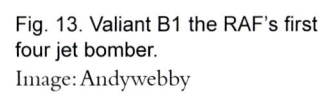

Fig. 13. Valiant B1 the RAF's first four jet bomber.
Image: Andywebby

Fig. 14. Victor Mk 2
Image: Author's own at Yorkshire Air Museum, Elvington

Fig. 15. The author with a Victor Mk2, a type that he flew when they were so secret they were not yet released to the RAF and it is now in a Museum!"
Image: Author's own at Yorkshire Air Museum, Elvington

Fig. 16. The author flying a Victor Mk 1, when they were very new, leading the RAF Aerobatic Team flying Hunter aircraft for a Photo Opportunity.
Image: Author's own

Fig. 17. Jet Provosts in formation.
Image: Author's own

Fig. 18. Folland Gnat.
Image: RuthAS

Fig. 19. Rapide
Image: Wikimedia

Fig. 20. The unique flight instrument panel in a Canberra.
Image: Bywat.co.uk

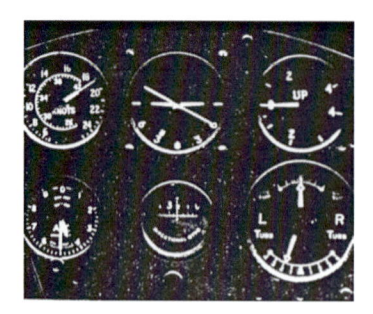

Fig. 21. Original Blind Flying Panel RAF 1930s.
Image: Author's own

Fig. 22. The original Gooseneck Flare used on Airfields
Image: Unknown

Fig. 23. Gooseneck Flares set as a Flare Path designating the Runway.
Image: Unknown

Fig. 24. The Attitude indicator on the Smiths Military Flight System where the attitude had to be inferred by interpreting a vertical pitch line and two roll lines, one either side going on opposite directions.
Image: Tangoprint

Fig. 25. An original Artificial Horizon operated by suction driven gyros.
Image: Author's own

Fig. 26. The "Classic Flight Envelope" showing the boundaries of operation for Altitude and G Force.
Legend:
Green 2G
Blue 3G (often BLACKOUT without practice of physiological aids - G suit etc)
Red 4G
Purple 5G
Image: Tangoprint

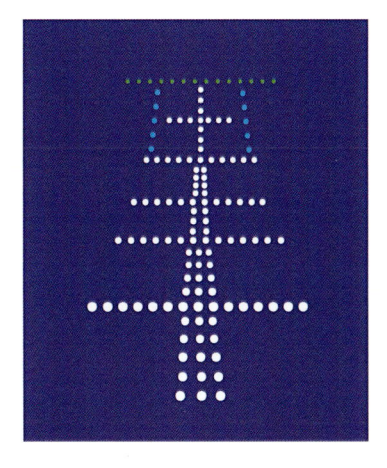

Fig. 27. This set of Calvert Approach Lights shows the direction of the runway and if the correct descent path is being followed the shorter cross bars, helping to orientate level, appear to the pilot as being a constant length across the approach.
Image: Tangoprint

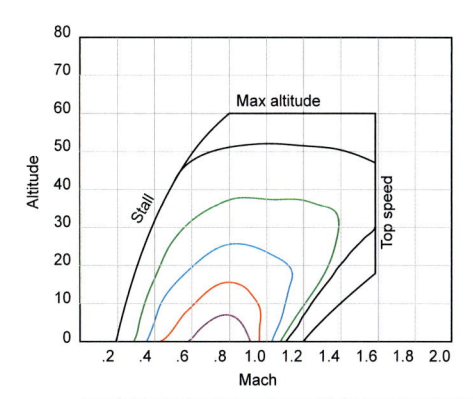

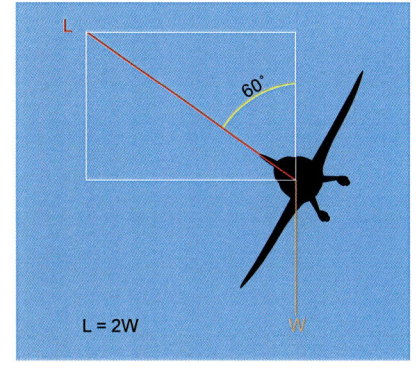

Fig. 28. To fly level and turn the aircraft banks and applies a larger force which can split between a vertical component to maintain height and a component into the turn to change direction. This larger force is felt by the aircraft occupants as an increase in weight and is measured in multiples of the weight felt when at rest – 1G.
Image: Tangoprint

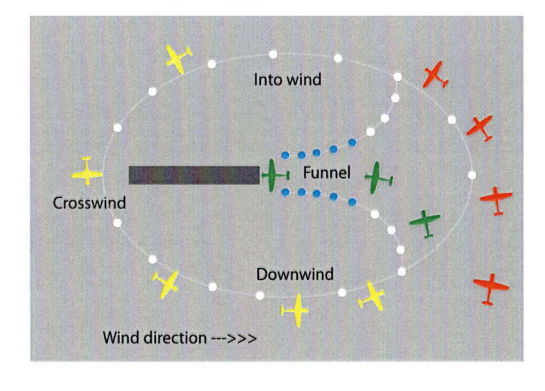

Fig. 29. Approach and Landing Pattern WW II and after into 1950s. Red symbols joining the pattern. Yellow let-down into wind on "Dead Side" and continue at 1000 feet around the Circuit.
Green is the descending turn into the Blue Funnels to approach and land.
Image: Tangoprint

Fig. 30. Boeing 707 - 436
Image: John M. Wheatley

Fig. 31. Boeing 720B
Image: Wikimedia;
Piergiuliano Chesi

Fig. 32. Concorde
Image: Eduard Marmet

Fig. 33. The Tobago TB10 used at the RAF Institute of Aviation Medicine for experimental flying during Performance change with Fatigue due to Sleep Loss.
Image: Author's own

Fig. 34. The author about to do the experiment in the Tobago TB10 after being kept awake all night!
Image: Author's own

Fig. 35. This WWII issue of the Fighter Pilot's Ten Commandments was still in use in the 1950s when flying Meteors.
Image: Authors own

Fig. 36. Certificate issued if you "Pranged" the Simulator on the Victor Mk1... I never had one issued!
Image: Authors own

a Canberra, conducting the event, had an opinion on that question. We had to wait for the reconnaissance photography to come back. The final judgment was that The Air Officer Commanding was not impressed with the accuracy of our bombing from Valiants!

BACK TO THE ROUTINE

Then it was back to the UK and re-configure the bomb bays for the Nuclear Role again. The pattern was doing long cross-country flights, navigating by star fixes and simulated radar bombing runs. Some were planned and some after being called to Readiness and a bit if a scramble. On the long trips we were supplied with in-flight rations consisting of a variety of sandwiches, chocolate bars and soup. There was a soup heater behind the pilot's seats and our Signaller, this was before the more grand title of Air Electronics Officer, would be in charge of heating that for the crew. Invariable some got spilled over his gloves and we were sure we could survive by stewing his gloves for days in the event we had to survive after a crash. My children enjoyed the chocolate, and the odd sausage for the cat, and my teeth took a hammering.

About now I was beginning to see less experienced Co-pilots than me being sent off to become Captains and to command their own Valiant. After some muttering and a bit of digging I learned that I had been selected to be a Captain on the first Victor Squadron, but there had been delays as there were problems with the Victors. They had been grounded! So, that was to be the next aircraft I flew operationally.

Chapter 10

Victor Mk 1

First flown 30th June 1958

CAPTAIN AGAIN

I was absolutely delighted to be made a Captain on the first Victor Fig.16 Squadron. It was the last of the V—Bombers to become operational. Although the shape was not quite as revoltionary as the Vulcan it flew higher and faster, on occasions some exceeded the speed of sound, Mach 1. I found that it really did handle like a fighter and was duly "arraigned" before the Wing Commander Flying at the OCU for flying it like a fighter. From the end of the Downwind leg, doing "Spitfire" continuous curving final descent and rolling out to touchdown on the runway!

SETTLING IN

The delays in the Victor coming into service were caused by some dramatic structural failures. The tailplane had come off an experimental aircraft while testing the aircraft configuration and then the same thing happened to a Victor prototype. The problem had been that the sums done to establish the strength needed to hold the tailplane onto the fin had not included the dihedral[39] of the tailplane. The fitting had to be strengthened on all the aircraft on the production line before they were released. So, we were now flying a concentrated Intensive Flying Trial to get hours on the aircraft to see how it settled into RAF service. The crews were delighted with the aircraft and the configuration for the Rear Crew was the same as the Valiant but they stepped down to the pilots' cockpit, instead of up as in the Valiant. That meant that they could look forward out of the front to see what was happening more easily.

PUBLICITY

Not long after the Squadron had settled in I found that the span of the Victor Tailplane was the same as the Hunter fighter. At that time the RAF Aerobatic Squadron was using Hunters painted completely black so I thought it would be a good publicity stunt to fly formation with them in an all white Victor. That was how I ended up leading the RAF Aerobatic Team for a photo shoot with them flying formation on my Victor. Their Leader never did get the message that it would have been more spectacular to formate on the Victor tailplane!

Another publicity flight was a "Ranger" flight to an overseas base carrying a newspaper reporter. All very correctly done with no mention of some of the more delicate equipment we were carrying. The embarrassing

---

[39] Dihedral is the angle of the horizontal stabiliser up from the horizontal.

bit was that we had a fuel problem on the way in to the base and had to spend half the night helping the Crew Chief[40] fix it ready for the next leg.

We always carried our own Crew Chief as part of the regular crew when we landed away. These Technicians were both highly skilled and very experienced to be selected for this job of Crew Chief. While originally this was seen as quite an honour, to be selected, it did mean that in V-Force we had a very high level of Technical Staff. When promotion time came around the Technicians on other RAF Stations did not have to be so exceptional to be considered for promotion – as above the general average on that Station. To add to the difficulty as Flight Sergeant level rank, Senior Technicians, the next level was Warrant Officer and that was generally an administrative post. It took a long time to sort out that problem.

EXCEPTIONAL PERFORMANCE

On one occasion when I was doing a training flight we found a Battle Formation of four Hunters flying at about 40,000 feet. They had no idea we were above and behind them so I dived down to their level, cruised past their Number 4 by a good margin of speed and pulled up in a climbing turn over their formation. The Victor could out-manoeuvre any of the contemporary fighters and when on detachment to Malaya we ran rings around the Royal Australian Air Force F86 Sabres at very high altitudes possible in the Tropical Atmosphere. Of course, at that time fighters were fitted with cannons and machine guns, in the days before guided missiles. They would not have been able to get a Deflection Shot[41] at a Victor, if our radar saw them creeping up on us.

FUEL AGAIN

On another occasion we had a fuel problem. We had been on another "Ranger" flight to visit the United States Air Force Strategic Air Command in North America. The Victor shut off valves in the refuelling system sometimes did not work immediately the tanks were full and so fuel would spill onto the parking surface. The Americans became very sensitive about the damage this did and insisted that we fuel the tanks using fuel gauges. This was so not to allow the Fuel Full shut off valves to operate on refuelling and prevent any spillage.

---

[40] He was in charge of the Ground Crew who serviced the aircraft – it was definitely "His" aircraft.

[41] The guns fired forward so when turning from the side of the target the aircraft had to aim in front of the target, deflection shot, for the bullets to arrive when the target got to that bit of sky.

We had been doing this each time we landed at a new base in North America and we ended up in Canada in readiness for the return flight to Base. At the Navigation Briefing it was clear that we would be close to a very strong Jet-stream on our route back to the UK. I thought this might give us a chance to break the speed record for an Atlantic Crossing at that time. We duly briefed to fly in the Jet-stream at about 0.93 Mach, which was about as fast as I wanted to cruise given the higher fuel consumption at high Mach Numbers. We set off in the rather bumpy ride in the Jet-stream and were going well and looking like a record was a distinct possibility. The Co-pilot and I were watching the fuel disappear at an alarming rate but the sums showed we still had a safe predicted reserve of fuel on arrival at Base. As we were looking at the fuel gauges they suddenly all fell back to zero!

Now, this was a bit of a problem because we had been filling up the tanks using these same gauges. The Crew Chief knew we had put in quite a bit of fuel into the aircraft but we had no idea if the gauges had been accurate at that time. So, goodbye record and I started a maximum range cruise to the nearest Master Diversion Airfield in South West England. We informed Bomber Command of our predicament and intentions and overlooked the North Atlantic ATC niceties to just get on with the job of considering ditching and parachuting procedures. There was a real danger that we would run out of fuel before we got to land again. However, we made it to the Alternate and went in to land from a high gliding approach. It turned out to be contaminated fuel in the works of the fuel tanks and a maintenance party had to come and overhaul the fuel system before we could get back to Base. That was a bit close.

ZERO, ZERO

I had another rather exciting trip one night on a Training Exercise. We had an electrical failure, not complete so the Flight Instruments were working but bad enough to return to Base. The weather at Base turned out to be Zero Visibility and Zero Cloud Base, so I asked for an Alternate with 1000 feet Cloud Base and 3 Miles Visibility. OC Flying demanded that I land at Base and made the order imperative to come to Alert Readiness. That was unusual but during the Cold War was taken very seriously. At any time of the day or night the Bomber Controller, who lived somewhere in a hole in the ground, might order the Force to come to a state of Readiness. The State of Readiness could range from crews just remaining close to the aircraft to sitting in the cockpit ready to take off. We came to be able to tell the state of Political Instability by the State of Readiness!

So, I made a plan to get down on the ground safely. The Co-pilot would fly the aircraft on the approach, and would use, as an additional aid to the instrument approach, the Zero Reader. The Zero Reader was an early sort of Flight Director fitted to the Victor at that time. I planned to take control at the last minute and land the aircraft. The Victor had an aerodynamic configuration that made landing it an easy and gentle process; some said it virtually "landed itself" as it came into Ground Effect. That was certainly going to help on this occasion.

Base was covered in a sort of drizzly fog with very little wind, so the approach on instruments was going to be smooth and I knew I could rely on the ability of my Co-pilot to put us in the middle of the runway, or thereabouts. In the early 60s we were just getting around to autoland capability and the Instrument Landing System at base had been calibrated with that capability in mind so I felt reassured as I began the approach. My main concern was the possibility of running off the end of the runway if I touched down too far down the runway, but neither did I want to crash into the approach lights. I had meticulously set the Airfield Pressure Setting on my Altimeter and we began the approach.

The Co-pilot did a first class bit of flying and we were on the centre of the runway, according to the Instruments, as we passed 100 feet. We were at the constant rate of descent on the Glide-path shown on the Glide Slope Indicator so I knew we would be aiming safely into the threshold of the runway. I still had no lights in sight when I said "I have control" and took over a perfectly stable and trimmed Victor. I started the flare as the altimeter went past about 50 feet and then there were the lights of the runway on either side of me, touched down and streamed the Brake Chute to stop well before the end of the runway. A nice bit of Crew Co-operation, but it was a bit close!

ANOTHER INSTRUMENT SURPRISE

I had another tricky bit of Instrument Flying in a Victor while doing a trial flight in the Cold War. The judgment was made that in periods of heightened political tension all the V-Force aircraft would be flown to more isolated airfields, in batches of four. In the event of an attack we would all need to get our four dispersed aircraft airborne from the dispersal airfield in four minutes. In order to do this we would have to start all four engines on the aircraft at the same time.

The Victor had an electrical start system on the engines so it was decided that a bank of many batteries linked together would be needed to give enough power to perform this unusual task. I was given the task of setting up a system of "Scramble Checks" to configure the aircraft at "Readiness" and to attempt to start all engines at once. We managed to get the engines to start together, and even accelerate at the same rate together to give full power.

The day came that it was now time to do a simultaneous start, as it was called, line up on the runway and take off with just enough fuel to land back below Max Landing Weight. We were sitting on a "Readiness Pan" just beside the runway and at an angle of about 45 degrees to the runway heading. The Crew Chief had a stopwatch ready to time the whole event and when he said "Go" we were off. The Co-pilot hit the start switch and all the engines began to wind up. I placed my hand on the nose wheel steering and throttles, moving the throttles gradually up to full power as the engines stabilized. We swerved onto the runway as the power came up to full take-off power and at our light weight were soon airborne.

The Cloud Base on the day was about 1000 feet and as we rocketed into it I looked down at the Flight Instruments – none of the gyros were working! None of the Gyro Instruments had had enough time to come up to operating speed before we entered cloud. I took off the power and eased the stick forward and we popped down out of the cloud. I did a low level timed circuit and landed a bit red in the face, we had some more planning to do for this "Four Minute Warning" procedure. A bit close, and egg on the face!

DOMESTIC HARMONY AND DISRUPTION

During this tour of duty I was living in a Married Quarter house on the Base. My Navigator lived next door and my Bomb Aimer just across the road, with my Co-pilot in a Quarter just round the corner. The final member of my crew, the AEO, lived in the Mess, but we didn't hold that against him. This was the first part of the Era in the RAF when crews wore Flying Kit all the time. It was even allowed in the Mess for the first time ever – a significant change to RAF etiquette! The Alert Siren would sound at any time of the day or night, and everyone shot off to the Operations Room for briefing. If we were at home then my crew would all emerge running from their front doors together and we were off as a crew to briefing.

Being so close to each other's families my wife took on the role of "Mother Hen" and supported and calmed the other wives of my crew, and became an expert "Counsellor". On retiring for the night I would leave my flying boots at the bottom of the stairs with flying suit and various items of clothing draped over the banisters up the stairs. If, and it sometimes did, the siren sounded in the middle of the night I was dressing as I descended the stairs and putting on my hat as I got through the front door.

On occasions I would leave the house in the morning expecting to be home for lunch, the Siren would go, we would disperse aircraft to remote airfields and the wives would not see us for, perhaps, ten days! Looking back I suppose it was a bit stressful but it was just part of the job at the time.

UNUSUAL EXPERTISE

While I was on this tour as a Victor Captain I took the opportunity to fly in the Rear Crew seat of the Radar Operator. My Co-pilot was being tested for his Instrument Rating by the Examiner, who was in the Captain's seat.

Having had a father who worked on Radar and TV repairs, in my teens I had worked repairing TV sets. A salutary lesson was to remember that about 4000 volts were still lurking in such devices even when just switched off. One test was to run the back of your hand along the TV chassis. If it was still "live" the involuntary response closed the hand to a fist and away from the shock. I had also studied Electronics at City and Guilds level and I rather liked to extend my experience. I had been involved with the Radar Operator when I was flying Valiants when we were doing "Target Prediction" work. Before we had any up to date photos of targets – we had at that time only WWII German Air Reconnaissance photos. The art was to guess what recent structures might have appeared around the target and how the radar returns would be presented. Anyway, I enjoyed the operating of the NBS in the Radar Operators seat, much to the surprise of my Navigator and AEO. I believe at the time I was the only pilot to "have a go" at operating the NBS equipment in the air.

Chapter 11

Victor Mk 2

First flown 17th May 1961

A PROTOTYPE CRASH

The Victor Mk 2 Fig.14. was a great improvement on the Mk1. The bigger wing and more powerful engines gave it a quantum jump in performance over the earlier version. The prototypes were being tested at A&AEE (Aeroplane and Armament Experimental Establishment) when one of them fell vertically into the sea at great speed and none of the crew escaped. This caused the aircraft to be grounded until the Royal Navy had recovered the wreckage and some analysis of the possible cause of the accident could be made.

Several possible causes were proposed and, because neither pilot had been able to use their ejection seat, lack of oxygen was considered. However, it was decided that the most probable cause was the failure of the pitot heads at the wing-tips had caused multiple flight instrument errors and runaway aerodynamic devices so that the aircraft became uncontrollable. It then probably entered a supersonic dive vertically into the sea where it broke up.

AEROPLANE AND ARMAMENT EXPERIMENTAL ESTABLISHMENT

Once the aircraft were again cleared to finish the acceptance trials "B" Squadron were short of pilots to complete the flying. On two previous years I had applied to go on the Test Pilots Course. On both occasions although my flying was deemed to be of the high standard needed at both interviews I was rejected because of an insufficiently good standard of mathematics. Ah well, I now found myself posted to "B" Squadron, with other experienced pilots, to fly some of the remaining acceptance trials on the Victor Mk2.

This was some of the most enjoyable and satisfying flying that I did in my whole career. Part of the testing was at very high altitude and very high angles of bank turning the aircraft as hard as it would allow. By this time the Russians had developed quite sophisticated Surface to Air Missiles (SAMs) and these manoeuvres were designed to escape from these SAMs. Fundamentally a SAM at this stage of development was limited aerodynamically. Although it flew at the high speed it was limited to quite a small rate of turn.

If a SAM was identified by Electronic Counter Measures as locked onto your aircraft, you could start a manoeuvre that made it turn at maximum rate to get ahead of you to catch you on that flight path. If then you could judge the range of the SAM, before it got to you, you could reverse the manoeuvre and the SAM at maximum rate of turn could not turn far enough to make contact with you.

This depended on the rate of manoeuvre of your aircraft so it was important to be at "the edge of the envelope" Fig.26. and in good practice.

The fighter/bombers in the USAF, as I recall being told, had a different ploy to avoid SAMs to ours. They would dive the aircraft until the critical moment and then climb violently to miss the SAM. Instead of vertical manoeuvre we were going horizontally by turning hard one way and then reversing the turn, all at maximum rate of turn. In the Victor Mk2 this was interesting because as you went through the stages of increasing "Stall Buffet", when you got to Third Stage it was really jumping about and shaking the wing-tips. Of course, at 50 odd thousand feet there was no G Force to speak of but it was a delicate operation nevertheless. It was no surprise that the Pitot Heads at the wing-tips had needed to be strengthened after the findings of the investigation of the crash into the sea, as described earlier.

SMITHS MILITARY FLIGHT SYSTEM

The Victor MK2 had a different instrument panel for the pilots from that fitted in the Mk1. It had the Smith's Military Flight System which was a military version of the flight system fitted to Commercial Airliners. The navigational display was excellent to fly along airways and easy to perform complicated instrument let-downs at civil airfields but that was not the sort of navigation that Bomber Aircraft performed! I was tasked with writing the notes to teach pilots and navigators how best to apply this kit at the OCU. A daunting task not only due to the complex switchery but also the complex power supplies to various bits of the System.

The Attitude Indicator, which was fundamentally an Artificial Horizon, had split attitude indications. Fig.24. The nose up or down was shown on a horizontal bar moving up and down the middle of the instrument. Meanwhile, the bank angle was shown by two bars, one each side of the instrument, moving in opposite directions around the edge of the instrument. See Fig. 31. To make it just a bit more difficult the rest of the flight instruments were not in the same pattern as the standard Blind Flying Panel. Fortunately pilots were used to doing mental gymnastics to interpret readings from flight instruments so using this kit was not as difficult as it sounds on first sight. However, there was a major problem because the nose up display bar only had limited vertical travel. Not a problem for a Civil Airliner but the Victor Mk2 at light weights and full power on take-off was heading more nose up than the indicator would show. Judicious use of the Airspeed Indicator and the Rate of Climb indicator were needed to get a stable climb during the take off and flap retraction phase of flight.

UNFORTUNATE CIRCUMSTANCES

Because of this rather unusual attitude definition on such a take-off it was easy to have the speed increasing to the Flap Limiting Speed before the flap retracted. This produced a marked airframe buffet as a warning to get the flap in and reduce the speed until it was done. These circumstances played a significant part during a night take-off for a Bomber Command Exercise.

On take-off just before 1000 feet, which arrived very quickly on this sort of take-off, a fire warning showed on an engine. The Co-pilot called No1 on fire but the Captain then corrected him by saying it was No2, instructing the Co-pilot to call the Tower and the Rear Crew to Put On Parachutes. During the engine shut-down drill the Co-pilot noticing the Undercarriage Flag operating told the Captain to watch his speed; the flag only operated at a speed below 160 knots with no undercarriage extended. At the same time Buffeting was felt which was the Pre-stall Buffet. I believe the Captain thought this was Flap Buffet and looking at the ASI misread the speed.

The two needle ASI[42] was now reading about 140 knots and the Flap Limiting Speed was about 240 knots, so this was an easy Human Error to make! He responded to the Co-pilots call to watch his speed by saying he was going for height and pulled the nose up even further, another indication that he misread the ASI. With no indication of his real nose up attitude on the Attitude Indicator, which was against the up stop, the aircraft reached a high nose position at the stall from which there was no chance of recovery.

Crews had an unwritten agreement that if things got really bad in a crashing aircraft then the Captain would punch the Co-pilot's left shoulder and say "GO!" This Co-pilot ejected and landed safely and was the only one of the crew to survive, and was able to explain the events.

GROUND TOUR!

When the trial ended I was sent to start the OCU for the Victor Mk2. I then had to write the Training Notes on the Victor Mk2 Systems for pilot training and run the Pilot Training at the OCU. So, this was what a "Ground Tour" was going to be like. At the time, I was one of the few pilots considered current on the Victor Mk1 and Mk2 and flew both on that posting.

---

[42] Airspeed Indicator; This one had a needle that performed one revolution for 100 knots, around a graduated scale, and a smaller on that read hundreds of knots around an inner scale.

Chapter 12

Piston Provost

First flown 12th August 1963

UPSIDEDOWN AGAIN

All pilots in the RAF who had done a Ground Tour were given a course of "Refresher Flying". After I left the Victor Mk2 OCU, the job of CGI[43] (Pilots), I was allowed to fly this aircraft to become familiar with the basics of flying once again. The Provost Fig. 2. was the current Basic Trainer.

I generally don't like side by side seat trainer aircraft but this was quite a nice aircraft to fly. Not too exciting but the engine was powerful enough to take it up in a vertical climbing roll and there was enough down elevator to perform an inverted flick roll – so it was fun flying for me. What I do remember most was that on each occasion after having been flying inverted there was a distinct smell of aviation fuel in the cockpit.

Being a tail wheel aircraft, a "taildragger", it was good to have to get the approach speed and attitude just right on the approach to get a smooth three wheel together touchdown. In a cross wind that is quite demanding and needs good control of the throttle to have, power off, rudder to get straight and aileron to level the wings. Good to get the coordination back and polished before going off to Central Flying School to become Qualified Flying Instructor.

---

[43] Chief Ground Instructor.

Chapter 13

Jet Provost

CENTRAL FLYING SCHOOL (CFS)

First flown 20th September 1963

This was the first aircraft I flew on the course at CFS. It was the jet version of the Piston Provost I had just flown on refresher flying, but quite different handling. Again the side by side seating was not my favourite but you could see what the student's hands were doing, and so stop him reaching for the wrong lever or button! I flew the Mk4 Fig.17. and even after all the improvements it did not fly in any sort of inspired fashion. It was pretty forgiving if mishandled so as a training aircraft it fitted that criterion. It was also very good at demonstrating the effect of having full or empty wing-tip tanks on the way the aircraft would spin.

So, I went through the teaching of the early stages of elementary flying. One of the manoeuvres we taught was a Turnback on engine failure at take off. Just after take-off a simulated engine failure would be called and the pilot flying would turn through 180 degrees to line up with the opposite direction on the runway to do a glide landing. In training this was usually done keeping the throttle at take off power, but it seemed to me that was unrealistic so I chose to close the throttle. As I hit the first stage buffet in the descending turn back to the runway the rather alarmed fellow student, who I was sharing the flight with, was shouting "You'll kill us doing this!" – Or words to that effect. But, I had the power coming back on as we rolled out and I saw no danger in flying to the limit – it was what I was used to doing. I didn't think it was at all close.

Chapter 14

Gnat

First flown 27th November 1963

ADVANCED FLYING TRAINING

Having completed the training at CFS on the Basic Trainer, Jet Provost Mk4, there were two options for aircraft for the teaching of the Advanced Training – the Varsity or the Gnat. Fig.18. Because I already had a tour of duty flying the Varsity it was a natural progression to go and fly them. However, the Folland Gnat was the first supersonic trainer for the RAF and had just arrived at CFS. I was eager to get my hands on one of those. I had an interview with the Commandant and talked my way onto an early course on the Gnat. Folland, the manufacturer, were generous enough to give the first QFIs[44] flying the Gnat pairs of Cuff-links in the shape of a small blue Gnat as a memento. I have mine still, and am very proud of them. Of course, these were not the only emblem of identification and the flying suit always had to have suitable badges sewed on. My wife became used to taking of old and sewing on new badges during my time in the RAF.

SUPERSONIC

The Gnat was small and sat close to the ground. When climbing aboard it almost felt like putting on a pair of trousers rather than entering a cockpit! Because the Gnat was an adaptation of the Midge fighter the rear cockpit had limited visibility. The rear pilot sat directly behind the front cockpit so most of the view forward was the back of the front ejection seat. Another innovation was that the flight instruments were up to OR946 standard[45], a roller blind attitude indicator, which was the same as those in the Lightning fighter. This attitude indicator was virtually unable to be toppled. The great trick was to make several specific and extreme manoeuvres so that as you went vertically up, it was showing vertically down! There is a good video of this roller blind presentation on YOU-Tube; searched for as Roller Blind Attitude Indicator. The Gnat was a "slippery" little aircraft with a comparatively high landing speed that needed a brake parachute to be used on landing. At the airfield being used by CFS at the time this meant that there was not enough runway available for a Gnat to land back just after take-off. Enough fuel had to be used to get down to the maximum landing weight for the runway length. It was a real pleasure to fly because you could squeeze the aircraft round the most extreme manoeuvres and keep it constantly in trim. It had a very complex operating system from the stick, in the cockpit, to the

[44] Qualified Flying Instructors.
[45] Operational Requirement 946; an attitude indicator to show all attitudes in pitch and roll without any errors
See Glossary.

"all flying" tailplane that made the transition to supersonic speed very smooth. This also meant that it could turn well at high Mach Numbers.
That annoyed some of the contemporary fighter aircraft when an occasional "turning match", when each was trying to get on the tail behind the other, happened to occur. The Gnat could get inside the turn and escape!

READY TO TEACH

After graduating at CFS I went off to an Advanced Flying Training school to teach newly graduated R.A.F Pilots about advanced flying in the Gnat. This was an interesting task and very rewarding as these chaps got the hang of the higher speeds and altitudes they were now subjected to in the Gnat. However, it was to become more interesting than I had expected on two occasions in this tour of duty.

A DAY TO REMEMBER

This trip started out like so many others, my student sitting in the front cockpit, as we climbed out of the misty lower layers of the air from the airfield. The only clouds were a few large cumulus clouds poking out of the haze, near a horizon of jagged mountain peaks. He was flying by instruments on this climb I was keeping a sharp lookout for other aircraft and monitoring his performance. As we passed into the darker blue quiet of the stratosphere, at 40,000 feet, he was performing well, turning onto a new heading, when the first of the problems arose. There was an Almighty BANG! I ducked and the visor on my helmet smashed on the stick. Wondering what was happening to the aircraft I looked up to see the student waving his arms above his head. Above his hands there was a large hole in the Perspex canopy that covered our two cockpits. The hole was right between our two ejection seats. My first thought was "Christ we've been hit…"

THINK QUICK!

All the air rushed out of our comfortable cabin with an explosive roar. I went instinctively into the Oxygen Drill – I could already feel my lungs being inflated as the pressure in my oxygen mask was increased by the regulator. I blew hard against this pressure deflating my lungs and letting them be recharged by the pressure I needed to stay alive. A couple of gasps and I had got into the steady rhythm of "pressure breathing". The noise started by the first bang had not stopped; there was so much noise that I could hardly think! The sort of noise from an aircraft at take-off power with reheat, if you are standing right beside it – it rattles your head and your chest cavity. Because of this noise, and the pressure of oxygen, I found I was not able to ask the student if he was hurt; nor could he speak to me. Now, this had all happened very quickly. The aircraft still seemed to be working, although the Central Warning System was full of flashing lights and sending a variety of alarm sound into my headset. So, I thought "Let's get this aircraft down to a height where we don't need "pressure breathing", where I can talk to him – and let's do it fast".

GET DOWN TO SAFETY

I rolled the aircraft on its back, closing the throttle and popping the air‑brakes I pulled her down into a steepening dive – a dive known technically as a Maximum Rate Descent. This is normally done just below the Speed of Sound but as the speed increased I felt the aircraft behave peculiarly in re‑sponse to my flying I decided to limit the speed to slightly slower than normal. To get a better rate of descent at this slower speed I went into a steeply banked continuous turn. As we spiralled down I checked around the cockpit again. It seemed to be behaving better now – no fire – engine and fuel OK – no malfunction in the hydraulics – it was looking good.

MORE PROBLEMS

About now I looked up from the instruments. The student had got his arms up again. He was securely grasping the face‑blind of his ejection seat. This blind pulled out above his head and down across his face to protect against air blast, and it fired the seat! "Oh God! He's going to eject!" The difficulty of communication was still with us because of the dreadful noise. If I shout "Don't Eject!" he might only get the "Eject" bit and he'll be gone. Now, the abandoning drill for the Gnat is quite clear that the occupant of the rear cockpit MUST leave first – otherwise he might not be able to get out at all! It crossed my mind that if I couldn't prevent him from leaving it might be a good idea to go first. Still, it seemed a pity to lose an aircraft because of this "Comedy of Errors" I shouted as loud as I could "Don't …" He tugged the blind – nothing happened! He had another go – these seats had been de‑signed especially for this aircraft and had never been used before. I ducked as the remains of the canopy flew off backwards, his seat fired, and away he went.

Immediately I felt as if all the Demons in Hades were shaking me by the head and shoulders. The buffeting effect of the airflow without the protection of his seat and what had been left of the canopy was hard‑ly changed by the small Perspex blast screen in front of me. It didn't help that my visor had broken so that the full air blast of about 400 mph was shutting my eyes almost completely. This stopped me from seeing enough outside to orientate myself. I could make out dim jagged shapes, but was that grey along the horizon a mountain or sky? Looking into the cockpit was no more help. My head was vibrating and the instruments shaking, so I was now unable to focus my eyes properly on any of the instruments.

DECISION TIME

Just as I was considering the situation my helmet tore off – now things were really getting difficult! "Where do we go from here?" I now have an aircraft which I can feel vaguely responding to the controls but I have no information to orientate myself and fly the thing "I can no longer control this aircraft – I'll have to get out after all!" I put up my arms to grab the firing face-blind on the seat, just above my head. I should simply pull the blind down over my face, for air-blast protection, and the automatics would work the ejection seat. I got my arms to about my chest before the airflow pulled them back; the right one outstretched and flailing to the right of the seat and the left one firmly held fast across my chest and neck. I just couldn't get to the firing blind! I had great trouble getting my flailing right arm back into the cockpit. Eventually I was able to grasp the flying suit with my left hand and help pull the right arm into the cockpit. I ended up in a crouched position with my hands in my lap.

The alternative seat firing handle, on the edge of the seat between my legs, was now right in front of my eyes. The airflow was still pulling at my shoulders and arms so I daren't sit up straight. Sitting straight backed is the approved position for ejection. The straight spine takes the kick in the pants, that takes you and the seat out of the cockpit, equally all along its length. I knew if I fired the seat in this crouched position some sort of back injury would result, but time was running out – this was my last chance! "I'll try to sit up as I pull the handle, that might work". I pulled the handle and started to sit up into the airflow. It came out about four inches on a bit of wire – "Oh God! It's not going to work"…BANG! Off I went out of the aircraft. One second I was thinking it wouldn't work and the next seat and I were tumbling head over heels through the air. There was still a lot of airflow but not nearly so much noise. Tumbling was not a good sign at this stage because the seat should have been flying quite stable, so I began to monitor the automatic functions as well as I could. I found out later that some of the seat mechanism had been torn off by the terrific airflow.

FREE FALL

My arms had been whipping round from front to back as the seat rotated, but my legs were held fast by the specially designed cords on the seat. As the seat tumbled over my arms came to the front. "Enough of this arm waving!" I managed to pull them in, cross them over and take a firm grip of my flying suit sleeves. They, at least, were now secure. I separated from the seat correctly. Toppling forward I kicked the seat away and felt my Stabiliser Drogue deploy. That was the first part of the parachute sequence and kept me in a stable descent. I realised I must be above 10.000 feet because the drogue would allow me to fall safely to that height where I would no longer need an oxygen supply. The oxygen supply that was supposed to feed into my mask that had departed attached to my helmet! I was now falling in my harness thinking "It's nice to be out of that noisy aircraft and in the quiet air". I had a look at the scenery because I could see the ground below me fairly well. It was mountainous scrub country but I could see no rocky outcrops. As I fell I was gasping and gulping like a fish out of water. Two things caused this: first, I should have been breathing oxygen and second, I was descending so fast that I continually had to keep clearing my ears by swallowing. I was just thinking "It's about time the main parachute opened" when there was a sickening swish as I went into "free fall!" "Oh God! I've fallen out of my parachute harness!" I had failed to realise that this would be the effect when the automatics released the Stabilising Drogue. I then had to fall some twenty feet before the static line opened the main parachute. I only had enough time to register the fright before "ZOT!" – the main canopy deployed. It came with such a thump that I thought, "I'll never be a father again!" I was then dangling, listening to all the country noises, floating down as prescribed in all the best manuals on the subject. I found that the supposedly solid back-plate on my harness had been damaged by the terrific air blast. This made it impossible to get my right arm up to grasp the harness for steering the canopy in the approved manner. Because of this, I was not going to be able to land in the correct manner.

TERROR FIRMER

As I came closer to the ground, I loosened my survival pack from my life-jacket so that it could hang down on the lanyard attachment. The pack formed a cushion in the ejection seat and had three attachments, one on either side of the life-jacket and one to a lanyard so it didn't float away from you if you had parachuted into the sea. It was very difficult on this terrain to judge the height from the ground, small clumps of bushes could be tufts of grass! As the survival pack hit I tried to do a sort of Judo break—fall and landed in a heap. I found myself, well winded, lying face up on a Welsh Mountainside. I felt rather thankful, if a little stiff and sore. The parachute tilted over on the rigging lines. Again, my training activated; I rolled over, reached up and collapsed the canopy by pulling the lines. I released the harness and found that I was feeling not at all well. I thought, "Must set out Ground Markers before I pass out". I crawled on my hands and knees in a circle, stretching out the red and white parachute canopy on the ground. I took off my life—jacket, pulled out the radio beacon and set it up very carefully. It was a standard bit of survival kit but it does work better if the antenna is aligned correctly. To make another bright object easily seen from the air I inflated my rubber dinghy. I had noticed some blood on my life—jacket. In one of the pockets was a heliograph signalling mirror so I took it out and looked at my face. It was a bit of a mess; cuts about the eyes and face from the visor, the whites of my eyes were both completely red and bloodshot and both eyes were well blackened. The overall effect was a grotesque panda—like appearance. I moved my finger back and forth, across and towards my eyes and I still seemed to have complete movement and depth of focus. This done I relieved a "call of nature" and inspected the lower parts of my abdomen. I satisfied myself that I was in pretty good shape really, so I could now relax. I lay down on the upturned dinghy "Oops!" Not too comfortable – something had busted in my back. That WAS close!

RECOVERY, FIRST STAGE

I had time to swat a couple of flies before a Welsh Sheep Farmer and his dog appeared. Having dissuaded his dog from giving me "First Aid" by licking some blood off my face, he told me that he had seen the two parachutes and the aircraft crash. We agreed that we should tidy up some of the equipment I had spread around and go down to his farm where there was a telephone. Fortunately, some of his friends turned up with a tractor. I rode "In State" sitting on my dinghy in a hydraulic shovel arrangement on the back of the tractor. When we got to the farm, my student was there already. I shook him by the hand saying, "I'm jolly glad you're alright but I didn't expect you to leave quite so suddenly!" It seemed that when the bang came he looked up and thought that I had been fired, in my seat, inadvertently out through the hole in the canopy. He then found the aircraft plunging earthwards, not responding to his efforts to fly it, so he thought it best to follow his departed instructor. After this event, a method of communicating between cockpits by waggling the stick was devised. That certainly worked, because further such canopy failures were experienced and safe returns made. Subsequently it was found that the canopies were scratched by refuelling hoses being dragged over them and weakened enough to fail under pressurization. However, in our case my Student had made an almost perfect ejection and descent safely. The student had already reported to Base and was now waiting for the rescue helicopter. That was able to home onto my radio beacon set up in the farmyard.

NOW RECUPERATION

The doctor from the helicopter had me strapped into a device that was more straitjacket than stretcher, and we were whisked away to Station Sick Quarters. You really do feel the inevitable vibration in a flying helicopter when you have a busted back!

From some x-ray photographs it was found that I had fractured vertebrae in my spine and some misaligned in my neck. I was fortunate not to have done more damage because of my posture when the seat fired and I was subjected to such large G forces. My right shoulder was strained but nothing was really broken except my back. A friend who came to visit me in hospital said I looked as though I had just lost a world heavyweight championship fight!

A few days rest in civil and military hospitals then off to Headley Court Medical Rehabilitation Centre for their efforts to get me back to flying.

NOW THE HARD BIT

Headley Court was a cross between a hospital and an officer's mess. Situated in beautiful grounds in the rolling hills of the Downs near Epsom it had been built as a Folly by some Regency Chap with a significant surplus of income. It had been donated to the RAF as a rest home for broken fliers. Added to the grounds was a fully equipped gymnasium, a heated swimming pool and a physiotherapy wing – not to mention the wards and occupational therapy rooms. There were patients from all three Services, foreign servicemen and ex-service people. There were all manner of ailments from simple broken bones, through strange diseases of the blood, unpronounceable things wrong with the bone structure to very odd complaints of the nervous and muscular system. It was all rather like an enormous, but first class, garage for human bodies.

WHAT NEXT?

I was determined to arrive there vertical rather than horizontal, so I went in a Staff Car instead of an Ambulance. Now began the real work of making my body perform properly again.

First came the inevitable thorough examination to pinpoint what needed to be done, before deciding on the treatment. I was to go into a class of patients known as "Spines". Most of my treatment was gentle, but very specific, exercise. This usually involved bending the opposite way to my crouching departure from my crashing plane. I had to build up the muscles in my back and shoulder, get my joints working, and get back to normal movement in body and limb. My exercises consisted of mainly lying down, on the floor of the gym working back muscles, under the lamp in the physio room, in the heated therapy pool exercising and in the glorious sun on the roof of the gym. The last bit during lunch breaks. Sounds easy, but the stretching and tensing of muscles and the manipulation of vertebrae and joints brings on a sweat quite quickly. There is something about the inmates of Headley Court; they are all pretty well broken, some in body and some a bit in the head from some trauma, but they are not broken in spirit. They all have the will to mend or adapt to a new way of life. Everyone there helps everyone else, but in no way condescending to those less able.

There is inevitably fun poked at the chap who falls off his crutches and the chap who drops his drink in the bar because his arm suddenly stops working. It was me that had the arm that didn't work. I found that when wearing a neck support collar then by pressing my chin on the right part of the collar it released the nerve that stopped the arm working – so I could get the drink safely to my mouth. The whole thing is looked upon as a mutual effort to get the patients back to a life as near normal as possible just as soon as possible. The Staff are magnificent. They give sympathy in a way which, although not goading, is still a spur to the patient. Coaxing him into further effort when he thinks he has reached his limit of ability without having to drive us!

Well, they did a jolly good job on me. I felt very fit, able to touch my toes and fall about, just about as well as I ever had. However, time is the great healer and I was not cleared to fly in an ejection seat for a few months after I left Headley Court. I spent my time doing various administrative jobs and exercising in the Station Gym. Exercise and games further strengthened my back making it completely supple again.

FLYING AGAIN!

When I started flying again because I had been away for several months, I had to go to Standards Squadron to be "retreaded". This was to make sure I hadn't forgotten too many of the tricks about how to teach Advanced Flying. It was going along quite nicely and I was enjoying the freedom of flying a Gnat again. About a week after I had started I was sitting in the Crew Room when I found there was a spare ride going. This was with a friend of mine, an Examiner at Standards Squadron, who wanted someone to sit in the front cockpit while he practiced instrument flying from the instructor's seat in the rear cockpit. I said that I would go along and without more ado, we were off. However, there was to be more to this trip than either of us could have imagined!

A DIFFICULT START

The airfield is on the coast and we had a bit of a gale blowing on that day. This meant that we were on the short runway taking off out to sea. Just after he got the aircraft off the ground, crossing the sea wall with the wheels still retracting, there was an Almighty BANG from the engine! The whole aeroplane shook. My comment was" Hey! I don't much like the sound of that…!" He agreed. We were now about 300 feet and still gaining speed. I scanned the instruments and said to him that I thought things didn't look too bad. We were not on fire and although we had lost power, there still seemed to be some thrust available from the engine. I said he had better throw us back on the airfield just as soon as he could. He already had the "feel of the thing" – a most significant factor in this sort of situation. It's known as "seat of the pants" feeling and it supplements the instrumentation both from the way the aircraft is handling and also draws attention to which instruments might be particularly significant. He was working hard to get us back on the runway, already doing landing checks.

As we came round the final turn to line up with the runway, I was expressing my approval when the engine coughed and stopped! We began to lose height at an alarming rate.

Now, ejection seats are very good and you can use them at ground level. However, if the aircraft is going down faster than the seat goes up and you are near the ground, you are not going to be on your parachute before you hit the ground. This was our predicament. I shouted, "Don't eject, we're stuck with it – if we bounce we can go…!" He had previously been in an ejection from a Gnat at ground level when he went out on a bounce during a crash landing so he knew just what I meant. One of the things taught at the AFS was a Practice Forced Landing, PFL, which involved having the engine at idle power and flying a specific pattern to, and over, the airfield and land. So, we both were well aware of the speed to fly, descent path and height to begin the landing flare. It was obvious now that with no engine and our height and distance from the start of the runway we were going into the undershoot!

A DIFFICULT END

We hit the ground, at just under 200 mph, out on the approach, with an Almighty smack in the edge of a small shallow stream. There was a deadly quiet and I wondered whether I was dead… I opened my eyes and found that the canopy was completely obscured by mud, as was the front windscreen. The grinding and crunching seemed to have stopped I began to think that we were bouncing, so if he can see out of the back we may be able to eject on the bounce. I decided, "If I hear him go then I'll follow". I'd had my knees bent so in the quiet waiting time I started to stretch them down to the rudder pedals when we hit again. There was an enormous crashing and banging and the front of the aircraft broke open. The instrument panel distorted, instruments broke up and grass and mud came into the cockpit, all around me and up to just above my waist. The jolting noise stopped. The stillness was broken only by a far off hissing and a quiet ticking.

He shouted, "Stop mucking about and get the hood open". The handle to do that was on the right of the cockpit wall, just forward and below my right shoulder, but it was under grass and mud! I pulled away the turf and

opened the canopy. He jumped out saying, "Come on, we're on fire!" A wing tank had a small fire licking out of it that looked rather nasty. "I can't move" I shouted, "I think my legs have gone or they are trapped". I couldn't see much further down than my waist because of grass and mud. He leaned over into the cockpit, undid my harness and tried to pull me out. I didn't move! I said "Clear off! This damned thing is going to blow up and burn in a minute". I thought, "What a way to die – survive the crash and then burn!" Muttering about where the fire wagons had got to, my friend climbed up the bank of grass that had brought us to rest.

RESCUE

The firemen, who had been exceptionally quick off the mark, arrived before he could climb to the top of the bank. My immediate thought was, "I hope they don't want to get me out of here by chopping off what is left of my legs!", but they didn't. They quickly put out the fire in the wing tank with a great squirt of foam out of the moveable spout on top of the driving cabin. Now started the real business of getting me out of the wreckage.

By now I had moved quite a bit of turf and feeling down into the mud found I still had legs down to about the knees. They felt a bit odd and I wondered if this might be the "phantom leg" feeling that some amputees experience. So, I thought, "From being about to die I was now fit for a wheel chair – things were getting better". Digging about in the mud, between my tummy and my left knee that pointed forward and my right thigh that disappeared into the mud, I discovered the toe of a shoe! Oops! That looks as though it's full of foot that has come off. I squeezed it. This was my left foot that I could feel, just in front of my left groin and with the sole towards me, toe pointing up! I found that I could still move the toes slightly, so the foot was still connected even if the leg was a bit smashed. The right leg was still a mystery, but by now, I was certain that there was enough leg for artificial limbs – another step forward.

SERIOUS DIGGING AND DISMANTLING

By this time, half the technical staff of the Station seemed to have arrived, to supplement the fire-crew and the medics. The M.O.[46] put a shot of something in my left arm while muttering something about my making a habit of crashing. As the firemen were cutting me out of the wreckage, they were supervised by the maker's representatives and our own technical experts. I recall particularly the manufacturer's representative hack-sawing away and a burly fireman tearing off bits of fuselage with his bare hands! They were all extremely gentle about the cutting and removing bits of aircraft until, at last, both my legs were free. My right leg was straight down into the wreckage. A hole was cut in the outside of the aircraft so I could move my leg out and back. It was then free of the bits of wreckage that pinned it down. An hour and three-quarters after take-off I was eased out of the wreckage and taken off to Sick Quarters. The house, Married Quarter's, that we lived in had Sick Quarters just across from the bottom of the garden. The Rescue Helicopter landed between the garden and Sick Quarters on several occasions with bodies in various states of injury. My poor wife, Moira, was forever looking out of the kitchen window wondering if it would be me coming out of the helicopter! My right leg had just a few holes in it but my left foot had been twisted off the bottom of my leg. The ankle and the next joint, between the ankle and toes, dislocated to twist the foot backwards and upwards. The Surgeon at the hospital specialised in injuries to mountaineers so I benefitted from his skill and expertise, then I was plastered from knee to toe. Now for recuperation!. That was close – too close for comfort!

---

[46] Station Medical Officer.

BACK TO HEADLEY COURT

The plaster had to stay on for about six week's altogether. I was then back to Headley Court again. There I was initiated to a group of patients in "Early Legs" and began more exercises to get my legs working properly again. Part of the strengthening of the leg muscles was to get back my balance and then learn to walk again.

Some of the doctors thought that my ankle would need to be "fused" and set immobile and that I might never walk properly again. However they were persuaded to wait until some rehabilitation had taken place before making the decision. There were several other Chaps limping around the place with various bits of surgery done to help, but I was determined to get to a stage where I could walk without a limp. Many weeks later, and having sweated and strained over my leg and foot, I did manage to walk and balance normally again.

Having learned to walk again, I was back to Flying Duties and instructing again. However, all was not well! While pulling 4 or 5G my neck would sometimes lock, and I would have to take the G off to make it work again. So, I was off back to Headley Court for more rehabilitation and assessment. The neck could not be fixed so it was no more ejection seats for me.

Off to Chipmunks again!

Chapter 15

Chipmunk, Again

FULL CIRCLE

Having started my flying career in the RAF, in 1951, flying the Chipmunk I ended my RAF career, in 1969, flying as a Flying Instructor, and Chief Ground Instructor, at a University Air Squadron flying Chipmunks – full circle of a career.

The first thing I found, when I arrived at the Air Squadron, was that it was taking three years to complete the Ground-school Syllabus and only two years to complete the flying. The poor students had to wait a year with virtually no flying before they could qualify for the Preliminary Flying Badge.

I convinced, with a presentation of new syllabus and teaching methods, the Hierarchy at Training Command that University Students already had experience in learning for exams. With a new teaching and a modified syllabus they could grasp the essentials and have a standard of understanding in two years. That would allow the award of the PFB as soon as the flying was passed. This method was adopted and went on to all the University Air Squadrons shortly afterwards. I wasn't sure the Boss would accept my proposed methods but I managed to convince him – but it was close!

Teaching flying at "Ab Initio" stage was very different to teaching Advanced Flying to pilots who already had qualified for RAF "Wings".
The students were from a variety of courses at the University and so had a wide range of knowledge and background. A student doing a degree in Aerodynamics could be briefed by a few diagrams and formulae on a blackboard but an Arts student needed much description and analogies to comprehend what we were trying to achieve. I would spend a long time just talking to a student to tease out his understanding of the various disciplines required to comprehend the science well enough. Then I knew how to use that knowledge to "speak his language" when teaching.
I had one student who could not seem to get the aircraft to fly down the approach properly. Great variations in height above and below the correct Glide-path were his main problem. Eventually I kept my hands lightly on the stick and throttle as he tried again to approach. I discovered that he was taking off power when it should have been increased. So I flew an approach and had him say "More power! or "Less power" as I wandered higher and lower on the Glide-path. He was right every time!

I then discovered that as an Agricultural Student he had been driving a tractor for the rest of the week and the throttle worked the opposite direction to the aircraft throttle. That problem solved he went solo.

I also found that many of the students had very delicate tummies! So much so that even after a steep turn they were sometimes sick.

Eventually I had a rubber stamp made that read "HE WAS THEN SICK"! One of my best students was completely set on going into the RAF, but unfortunately he had much use of my rubber stamp. Eventually I persuaded him that his place was in an Airline Flight Deck and not a Fighter Cockpit. I met him some years later as an experienced Captain, flying for a prestigious airline and he was very happy in his chosen career.

A BIT OF EXCITEMENT

At a time well before the present day's rigorous flying discipline was applied, many occasions arose for "showing off" the abilities of your aircraft. On one such occasion I was an Instructor taking up a Student for the first flight of the day. Years before it had been a tradition that if you could catch the aircraft at another airfield on the ground, before their first flight of the day, you would "beat up" their airfield. This involved making fast low passes at various angles of bank and possibly even upside down during a roll!

On this particular day the weather was what a Met Man would call Warm Sector conditions, low cloud with good visibility below and no rain. Not the weather when I could teach my Student anything much at his level of ability – not yet ready for instrument flying. So, I took the opportunity to fly over to a local airfield where light aircraft operated and I knew the Airfield Manager who was an old friend and retired RAF pilot. I proceeded to beat up the airfield and flying past the Control Tower at about the height of the windows pulled up into a loop. As we got towards the top of the loop we entered cloud. Now, I always made sure when I flew a loop I ended up at a height greater than that at which I had started – always gain height in a loop. However, as we went over the top of the loop I realised that today I had full fuel tanks and a very large heavy Student in the front cockpit. Upside down, in cloud, zero G and a toppled Artificial Horizon[47] – don't panic! I wasn't going to see the ground until we came out of cloud pointing straight, or near enough straight, down.

[47] The Artificial Horizon is the main flight instrument to show pitch and roll attitude of the aircraft.

I really had to get the ultimate performance out of this Chipmunk to ensure we did gain height in this loop.

I reduced the throttle to about one third as we started down, pulled quite hard on the stick until I could just feel the airflow starting to break away from the wings – giving maximum lift and drag "on the nibble", as it was known. Having come out of cloud, as we were pointing about 45 degrees down I came up to full throttle maintaining the "nibble" and we gained about 50 feet. I roared away waggling my wings, with an increased heart beat and "with my tail between my legs". Fortunately, like all students, my student had complete confidence in my ability and was not "put off" by the experience, but that was a bit close!

AN OFFER I COULD REFUSE

Before I had my first accident I had been approached by Senior Staff Officers from Bomber Command to see if I was interested in being involved in the flying training at the OCU for the new aircraft, the one that became the Tornado.

By that time I had seen enough of new aircraft being introduced to know of the problems to be faced. The Politicians defined the task, a design was approved, RAF Officers were allocated on a two year tour to supervise the construction and development and the aircraft appeared at the OCU. Sometimes the next two year tour Officer at the factory had quite a different idea from his predecessor and that caused delays.

As an example the keyboard to operate a new Flight Simulator had been designed with an "alpha numeric"(like today's mobile phone keyboard) arrangement, but the next chap said "We are now all Computer Literate, we need a "qwerty" keyboard." An enormous amount of work on wiring and software entailed to make the changes at the factory. This was just one of the delays that could occur in the ten years, or so, from design to introduction on an aircraft.

Aircraft never seemed to be designed with enough internal fuel, so the first modification was always to start to find places to hang more fuel tanks on the aircraft.

That would be followed by a change in task, so different or modified weapons would have to be attached somewhere on the aircraft. By that time a new design might be accepted only to be scrapped by the next set of Politicians before it could be introduced to service. TSR 2 was a classic example of this process.

I decided that I would leave the RAF at the end of my current engagement. If I could successfully make the transition from RAF Pilot to Airline Pilot the financial security of my family would be better served. So, the University Air Squadron was to be my last Tour of Duty in the RAF.

BACK TO SCHOOL, AND DIFFERENT FLYING

While I was at College learning about Civil Flying and the examinations for the Airline Transport Pilots License I was approached by some very interesting people offering employment. One chap was offering a well paid job flying into and out of Russia – this was 1969 so the U2 flights were long gone! I guessed it was still Air America so I declined. Another had a job flying fighters on offer – in the middle of Africa somewhere!

By now I was more interested in finding a way to settle down with, and financially support, my family. Airlines seemed much more likely to provide the security I was looking for to support the family in the manner they would like to be accustomed.

Chapter 16
Boeing 707-436

First flown 2nd May 1970

BOAC FOR BEGINNERS

Having now achieved possession of an Airline Transport Pilot License and an Instrument Rating I was looking for a job. I was accepted to become a pilot with British Overseas Airways Corporation, the long range flag carrier for the UK airlines.

BOEING 707-436

BOAC had decided to have the American Boeing 707-436 Fig.30. as well as the British Comet aircraft on their long range fleet. The only advantage it had over the Comet was in greater range, and the take-off performance was not as good. Pilots flying the Comet, and the later VC10, joked about the early 707 that it "only got airborne due to the curvature of the earth", because of the long take-off run.

As is often the case, the flying controls were designed to fit the test pilot assigned to development of the aircraft. Tex Johnson was a big chap and my little hands had some trouble fitting onto the control yolk to fly the aircraft without also pressing some of the buttons on it. The 436 had Conway engines, which I was familiar with from the RAF, but with thrust reversers which were new to me. The flying controls were a bit heavy but responsive enough and asymmetric flight did not give rudder loads that were too high.

I converted to this type of aircraft just as there was a move to change take-off procedures to climbing out at V_2 + 10 knots. I must have been one of the first in a 436 to fly this new technique as we went off to our training airfield for a practice session. The aircraft was very light, no passengers or freight just a handful of pilots for training, and at the time take-off was always at full power. I appeared to be looking straight up over the aircraft nose as we used almost no runway and shot up at a very extreme angle. Strange that if we used the old methods of operating the take-off path today, of full power and staying low until the best climbing speed was gained before climbing we would be in trouble. No less than if we had used today's techniques, climb out at V_2+10 and less than full power(to reduce the noise), long ago we would have been thought to be hazarding the aircraft!

MORE NAVIGATION

Having converted to the aircraft as a Co-pilot, I was surprised to find I was now to be trained as a Flight Navigator. Although I had been a Staff Pilot training Navigators in the RAF the role of Flight Navigator in civil flying was rather more complex. Lots of sums, spherical trigonometry, astronavigation computation, long range radio aids and how to conjure up a position line out of thin air! The periscopic sextant poked up out of the top of the pressurized cockpit, now called a flight deck, and a small stand had to be use to help you reach the eyepiece for star shots. Having passed the theory, the practical tutoring was a bit of a shock.

While in the RAF I was used to at least an hour briefing and preparing charts and logs. Just grabbing the route and Met Forecast from Operations and trying to prepare the chart and do the sums for headings and ETAs in the aircraft, taxed my speed and accuracy compromising somewhat! All this was being done while we did checks and taxied to prepare for take-off. However, with a little practice and application I got to grips with the technique well enough.

MOONSTRUCK BY NAVIGATION

We were "down the route" (as being away from Base was known) in the North Pacific when we picked up an aircraft to go to a remote island in the South Pacific. The weather was remarkably good for the area we were to fly and we were soon on our way. I then noticed there was a discrepancy between the two compasses. I asked the Captain to check on the Magnetic Standby Compass and it was not clear which of the two was correct. There was definitely something very odd going on. Eventually the problem was solved and now I had to find out where we were. I went back to do some sums for a three star astro fix. This involved pre-computing where you would be some time later and calculating where you would be for the first two star shots. Having got the position lines from all the shots, by moving the information together to the final shot you had a fix. Well, that usually worked, but this time it was rubbish and I was having trouble identifying the unfamiliar stars in the Southern Hemisphere. I computed for another fix well ahead and tried again. Still rubbish, and we had now been going for some hours across the ocean. I decided to go forward between the pilots and look out at the sky to see what stars I could recognise. There was the Moon, so I could now get a good first shot on the Moon. No trouble finding that in my periscopic sextant and that had about a 7 degree visual arc. I also spotted to the North a star of bright magnitude that was visible from the Northern Hemisphere so I had used that before. I did the sums, shot the shots, got my fix and breathed a large sigh of relief. We could now set a proper course for the island and, at the very least, get within range of their navigational beacon. That was close, and a bit uncomfortable!

Chapter 17

Concorde

CONCORD EVALUATION TEAM

Yes, that was the original spelling! Because I had done some flying doing trials at A&EE at Boscombe Down, the BALPA[50] team asked me to join them while Concorde Fig.32. was being developed.

This was the Concord Evaluation Team made up of experienced Airline Pilots who were likely to fly the aircraft on the routes being planned. This involved meetings with the designers and test pilots, as I had done with the Victor Mk2, and much discussion on flight profiles and reserve fuel policies.

It involved flying the simulator in a variety of profiles and failure modes and flying the aircraft for experience. The simulators that we used were at Toulouse and Filton with the flying done out of Filton. The aircraft was a delight to fly and very manoeuvrable – so much so that one pilot from a foreign airline got very close to the structural limit on demonstration. This resulted in the "stick forces" being increased to give more of the feel of a large airliner. Some might say that the change was rather over done because later a pilot damaged his foot on the rudder due to the higher forces.

It was particularly stable on the approach, as large delta wings are, and that gave it a good chance of landing in poor weather conditions. Although it was stable in pitch on the approach there was quite a nose up attitude so at the flare you were well above the runway. There was much discussion and calculation before the amount of "Droop" on the nose was decided upon because of this nose high attitude in the flare.

The various automated flying control enhancements all played a part in the smoothness of operation. If those were taken out and an approach made on asymmetric power, with a pair of engines on one side closed down, and auto stabilization out it became a bit more difficult. I tried this in the simulator and experienced the difficulty for myself. But these were conditions that were very unlikely to occur.

Some of the airports were not very pleased with the noise that the four afterburners[51] on Concorde made on take-off. So, some quite exciting manoeuvres had to be executed just after take-off, to pacify the inhabitants surrounding the airport. A fairly steep climbing turn at full power just after the wheels retracted had to be executed to miss the sound recording units that had been strategically placed to measure the number of decibels!

---

[50] British Airline Pilots Association.
[51] A device to inject fuel into the jet engine efflux so that it burned to give extra power, and a long sheet of flame out the back.

As ever the cockpit and flying controls were configured to suit the Senior Test Pilot so the throttles were well back and quite difficult to get my little hands around all together. The flight instruments were mostly conventional but with a slightly unusual layout. The Rate of Climb and Descent meter was replaced by a Vertical Speed Strip Indicator, but it was situated to the right of the Artificial Horizon as usual. The rest of the instruments you could have found in most airliners of the day, with the exception of a Mach meter that read just over Mach 2, a C of G meter and a skin temperature meter.

The Flight Engineer returned to the cockpit after having been relegated from the new Two Pilot aircraft and he was an essential part of the team. A large part of his duties was to move fuel around the tanks to maintain a stable C of G as the aerodynamic forces changed through the range of speeds operated on climb, cruise and descent. He also monitored the Engine Ramps in the air intakes. These automatically produced Shock Waves in the air intakes to reduce the airflow from Mach 2 to about Mach 0.65 so that the engines could operate normally.

The old rules for Fuel Reserves were extensively modified to suit the small amount of fuel left after an Atlantic crossing, but the effect of changing wind patterns was not so great at Mach 2 so that made the end result more predictable. A system of adjusting arrival time while still out over the Atlantic was devised to enable Concorde to fit into the arrival pattern without much delay. It became quite usual to land with fuel reserves much lower than had been the accepted norm for many years.

It should also be remembered that the aircraft had to pass certification that made it suitable for the "Average Airline Pilot" to fly and the speeds on the approach were able to fit it in amongst other traffic easily.

However, it was difficult to get flying time on the available aircraft because often either the weather was too bad or the aircraft was unserviceable. A very frustrating time; so I had to wait to be a passenger to truly experience Mach 2, although I had been up at about 60,000 feet in the RAF.

Just at this stage of development I came to be offered a Command Course on the Boeing 707, which I was currently flying. Quite a dilemma; do I wait for a Co-pilot Course coming soon on the Concorde or do I go now for a Captain appointment on the 707. After much hard thinking, deliberation and soul searching I decided that this time I would forego my selfish love of flying the latest aircraft and put my Family Finances first. A pension as a Captain would be a major increment above a Co-pilot and, anyway, it would be nice to be "in charge".

Chapter 18

Boeing 720B

First flown 18th May 1972

When it came time for me to be promoted to Captain it was found that the CAA[48] did not think I had enough flying hours on Civil Aircraft. I was therefore "Seconded" to a small independent airline that operated Boeing 720 Fig.31. aircraft. The cockpit, controls and aircraft systems were virtually identical on the 720 to the 707 that I had been flying, so conversion was no problem. The great thing was that the 720 was shorter and lighter than the 707 but had the same engines so the performance was much better. Better apart from range where to get to the Caribbean from UK we had to refuel at the island of Santa Maria, in the Azores.

Operating in a small airline was very different to being part of a huge operation! The crews came to know each other, and what kind of operation to expect when flying together. The work was allocated on a Roster system that used a "rolling 28 days", so that you always knew what you were doing for the next 28 days. Quite different from the Calendar Month allocation of work I had come from where towards the end of the month you had no idea what you were in for next month!

The destinations we operated to were mostly Mediterranean island and coastal resorts, and occasionally to the Caribbean islands. We carried a Flight Navigator for the ocean crossings and one was surprised to find that his Co-pilot was a current Examiner of Flight Navigators – much hilarity!

I quickly became aware that "the locals" in our destination ATC were not going to use the International Language of English to their own airliners. Thus, I became adept at knowing the salient foreign words, height, heading, level, climb, descend and the numbers, to tell me where the other aircraft were and what they were doing. Essential in an environment where the locals would be able to dart into the flight path to get into the airfield, I was aiming at, in front of me and thus cause a delay for my passengers.

The crews were a friendly bunch and highly skilled in their operation and that made my tour with them most enjoyable. The Company did ask me to stay and take a Command with them, but I decided to take a Command with British Airways as a safer bet. There was a difficult time ahead for smaller airlines.

---

[48] Civil Aviation Authority.

Chapter 19

Boeing 707-336

First flown 2nd April 1972

The 707–336 was very similar to the –436 but it had engines made by the American company Pratt and Whitney. Their engines were a bit more temperamental than those on the –436 and required more gentle handling. However, they did burn less fuel and so gave the 336 a greater range. This was the type I flew to the end of my time with the airline that had, in the meantime, become British Airways. That was an amalgamation of BOAC and BEA, British European Airways, the short haul flag carrier for the UK.

WHAT TORNADO?

Eventually, I was promoted to Captain and had command of my own aircraft again. Being overseas in command of an airliner was very different from being overseas in command of a V-bomber. When in the RAF I could pick up a phone and make things happen, getting priority spares and service. In an airline there seemed to be layers of bureaucracy and to get things done I had to be very firm or just get on with the job myself.

On just such an occasion I was on a flight from UK to a destination on the East Coast of the USA. The weather was not unusual but quite thick cloud up close to our cruising altitude. There was a large depression, complete with trailing fronts just a few miles inland, but there were no reported problems of airports having unusual delays. The whole let-down was in cloud but there was no unusual turbulence. We were handed over to the airfield Radar Approach Director from the Area Controller at about 3,000 feet and made ready for the approach. The Approach Controller said "We have a Tornado in the vicinity, the Tower has been struck by lightning, there is a very strong crosswind and the last aircraft to approach all made Missed Approaches. You are number four in the pattern, what are your intentions?"

DECISION TIME!

I was carrying standard fuel, that meant I had enough to go to the Alternate Airport, and even then hold for 30 minutes before landing. I immediately opted to divert to the Alternate and asked for clearance to proceed there.

I was given a heading to fly and climb to 5,000 feet with a change of frequency to Area Control. Area Control gave me a clearance to "Climb and maintain 7,000feet". I asked when I could expect a climb to cruising altitude on the way to the Alternate. I was told not to expect any further climb from 7,000 because of other traffic.

This meant two things; I was going to be short of fuel and there was likely to be a long time to hold at the Alternate. At 7,000 I would be using something more than twice as much fuel as at the cruising altitude planned for the diversion. We were in danger of running out of fuel!

A BETTER SOLUTION

I looked on the chart at the route from my Destination to the Alternate and quickly noted that not far along the route, and fairly close to it, was another airport used by my airline. I decided to go there, if they would have me! I told the Co-pilot the plan and he retorted in amazement," We can't go there we don't have the let-down charts for that airport!"

By this time we must have been getting close to the Tornado. The cloud was very lumpy with the aircraft occasionally jumping up and down, with the wings visibly flapping up and down and with the engines gyrating as if they were about to fly off the end of the supporting strut. I said" Forget about the paperwork, just look up the frequency for the airport and ask them if they will take us." He did, and they would!

His next problem was how to find information on the landing aids available. He reiterated, "We don't have any Approach Charts for this place!" I said "Just ask the Approach Controller for the ILS[49] frequency, the Runway Heading, the Safety Height and a heading to intercept the Localiser." Having set the information that he obtained we carried out an almost normal approach and landing at the chosen airport.

As we taxied in to the Terminal we could see other aircraft refuelling, so that was the next challenge. The Flight Engineer and the Purser both did a great job in persuading the refuellers to put enough into our tanks to get us back to the Destination. I went off to the Tower to get an ATC Clearance and sort out the Administration needed for our surprise visit. I then discovered that I had the Airport Manager for our Destination as a passenger and he was very impressed and helpful in achieving our aim to get to the Destination before my crew ran out of Flying Hours.

---

[49] Instrument Landing System: a radio beam along the runway and another up the approach path — See Glossary.

BACK TO THE DESTINATION

All went well and we were away from the Alternate and back to a damaged but operating Destination in record time, much to the delight of Crew and Passengers. So, the day was saved! We did not run out of fuel, when faced with an impossible flight path to the Planned Alternate, and by cutting through the bureaucracy of Cockpit Paperwork landed safely. Getting refuelled and to the Destination was a very satisfactory bonus – but it was close!

SURPRISE IN THE SOUTHERN HEMISPHERE

One of the natural things for an Airline Pilot to do is to consider which runway and departure procedure might be used while travelling from the hotel to the airport. I was doing this as I was on my way from the hotel to an airport in the Southern Hemisphere. I was quite comfortable with my plan until I got to the Briefing Room.

I had planned for the reciprocal runway! Being south of the equator the sun was in the Northern part of the sky and not what I was used to – in the Southern part of the sky. Having realised how easy it was to become disorientated I recalled some historical navigation myths that I had read about.

When sailors first sailed across the equator from Europe they were mystified by a strange orientation of the sun and earth. In the Northern Hemisphere watching the sun it appears to travel from left to right as it climbs in the sky, but never appears overhead. Once well south of the equator in the Southern Hemisphere, where the sun travels across the sky but does not reach overhead, the sun appears to travel in an arc from right to left!! Some were convinced that in that part of the earth the sky rotated the opposite way to the Northern Hemisphere! The Human Mind will often find a way to play tricks on us.

Chapter 20
Dragon Rapide DH 89

First flown 10th December 1968

NOSTALGIA PERSONIFIED

The Rapide Fig.19. was a delightful 1930s aircraft that was a joy to fly. The pilot sat in a single seat in the cockpit right at the front of the aircraft. So, a check pilot had to be fairly confident of the candidate to let him fly the aircraft in the various configurations for the check. You really did feel how it was to be flying at the beginning of passenger carrying operations in the UK. Having a tail wheel it could swing on landing so it was an aircraft demanding attention until the landing was completed. Getting it to land on three points was a bit of a trick with quite a high attitude in the flare but I managed it on most occasions.

PARACHUTISTS

The purpose of my qualifying on the Rapide was to be available to drop parachutists for training and events, like garden parties or air shows. I would pick up the aircraft at the airfield where it was hangared and fly over to the airfield where the jumpers were based. There would then be a briefing and they would be loaded in dropping order. I would then take them off to the DZ, Dropping Zone, and they would stream out of the aircraft. I would do several loads on the day and the local DZ was not far from the airfield.

BUSY DAY

On one particular day I was very busy. The fuel gauges on the Rapide were the same old ones fitted to the Oxford that I had trained on. They were notoriously difficult to read because the single button select-ing each tank had to then be pushed firmly to get an accurate reading. The gauge reading also varied depending on the attitude of the aircraft, so it was all a bit "Hit and miss"! I had been keeping track of fuel reading through-out the day but by well into the afternoon I was suspicious that the gauges were not really showing me how little fuel remained. Although there was a satisfactory reading on the gauges I decided that after the next drop I would refuel The amount of fuel put into the tanks was the maximum capacity of the tanks! There wasn't much left in the tanks – that was a bit close.

Chapter 21

TB 10 Tobago

First flown 2nd March 1982

TO HELP PREVENT SURPRISES

Towards the end of my time with British Airways I was in a curious position. The Boeing 707 was being replaced by Boeing 747 aircraft. This was bigger and better, the first "Jumbo", and offered better flying schedules for pilots and better salaries, argued on better efficiency from the operation. Since we now had many senior pilots from what had been British European Airways, with my seniority I stood no chance of getting a Jumbo Command. So, how was I to be employed?

RAF INSTITUTE OF AVIATION MEDICINE

At the time there was an arrangement for pilots from BA to take part in experiments run by the Institute. These were at the Department of Flight Skills and involved measurement of reactions to displays and controls and evaluating alert and warning methods. At this time it did not involve any flying but a flight simulator was used to evaluate some tasks. I became involved in helping to design some of the tasks and I was told by BA I would probably be able to spend the rest of my BA time at RAFIAM. BA had too many pilots at my level and seniority and I was unlikely to get a Jumbo in the time I had remaining. This was to be another very rewarding flying time in my life.

SLEEP AFFECTING PERFORMANCE

Besides being involved in writing "Learned Papers" and designing computer databases I was also involved in flying a fully Airways Equipped TB 10 Tobago Fig.33. The experiment was to have several volunteer pilots fly a navigation pattern while performing designed tasks. Then keep them awake all night before repeating a similar flight. This was done in the aircraft and in the flight simulator. The simulator was rigged to match the performance of the aircraft. When I saw the flight profiles proposed by the scientists I was immediately able to say that they were far too exacting for such an evaluation. I then produced some modifications to their profiles and flew them with all the measuring kit fitted to me.

The kit included continuous measurements of blood pressure, heart beat rate and brain activity – unusual for pilots! The pilots would have all the airways navigational radio aids and would be flying only on instruments throughout. During the flight they would navigate to turning points, giving an ETA, change cruising altitude, perform specific tasks, and end with an instrument let-down and GCA (Ground Controlled Approach).

CONSULTANT TO THE CIVIL AVIATION AUTHORITY

By this time I had struck up a very effective rapport with the Senior Scientist in the RAFIAM Department that had now become known as Psychology Department instead of Flight Skills. So, when I took early retirement from BA I was offered a chance to carry on with the same job at RAFIAM as an Aviation Consultant to the CAA. What could be better!

We had a number of volunteer pilots for the trials of "Sleep Deprivation" experiments, mostly on loan from BA. I always flew as Safety Pilot, having checked the volunteer out as familiar with the aircraft. I also kept a log and continual evaluation of his performance. All the subjects were current Airline Pilots in good flying practice. I did the same in the flight simulator. The pilots then remained on the base and were monitored by a scientist to keep them awake all night before performing the next day.

NO REAL SURPRISES

As we expected there was a measurable deterioration in the performance of every pilot after being kept awake. There was some variation between pilots that seemed directly related to ability and experience. All the GCAs were flown perfectly adequately showing that when concentration was needed the instrument flying ability was the last skill to be affected.

However, in all cases there was a marked deterioration in the level of ability to perform peripheral tasks, even navigation suffered. The amount of deterioration seemed to depend on the level of importance allocated to the task by the subject pilot. The Senior Scientists gave a Learned Paper on these results to a conference in Helsinki.

OTHER RESULTS

I noted at the time that there was a measurable difference between the results a subject obtained in the aircraft to those in the flight simulator, although similar in nature each time. We thought that this might be an effect of a "Fear Factor" when not actually up in the air.

This difference is sometimes overlooked by researchers when flight simulators are used without a comparison to results in an aircraft. Another effect that is sometimes overlooked is that these pilots may not be "Average". They are confident enough of their proven ability to allow themselves to be given a flying challenge outside their normal environment and have their performance judged for research.

Having said that most airline pilots were sometimes required to fly without normal sleep patterns, but probably had never realized the effect it had upon their performance.

The bit of the brain that we use to measure our performance is, unfortunately, one of the first areas to deteriorate with fatigue. So, we don't know how badly we are starting to perform when fatigued.

BROAD RANGE OF RESEARCH

RAFIAM had done over many years research into effects of fatigue from a variety of sources. This small experiment was added to the total. Military and Civil aircrews helped the data to be collected and collated, sometimes in co-operation with NASA, to give a better understanding of the effects of fatigue on Human Performance.

Some of the work I was involved with was the construction of Questionnaire for research and also the construction of databases for research data. Databases turned out to be fascinating. I found that a very important part of their construction is to know how to find a way to retrieve sets of significant data before you start building the database. If that process is left out of the build of the structure it is hard to then find ways to "mine" the data effectively.

Later I became very involved with the Confidential Human Factors Incident Reporting Programme (CHIRP). This was a place where Pilots could report near accidents or close shaves with no fear of attracting blame. It had been found that when accidents were being investigated there had almost always been a previous event similar to the accident that had not ended in disaster. It was these previous to the accident events that the Programme was designed to capture.

When Pilots phoned in about their concerns and report events I was invariably able to say "Yes, I've been there …" and through such rapport gain their confidence. That allowed me to discuss much more detail than a straightforward report of an event.

I hope my small contribution helped because I found it most enjoyable. I also hope that the research pointed to new ways of operating so that there not be so many "surprises", brought about by fatigue, in the future of aviation.

THE DOWN SIDE

During the testing for one of these experiments I was wired up with all the medical parameters of interest for a record of my reactions. Next day I was approached by a Scientist from Physiology with some bad news. He had found that I had a non-standard heart and that had to be reported to the CAA! So, my licence was immediately revoked and a series of tests and reviews by eminent Heart Specialists, both part of the CAA and Harley Street, ensued. Eventually the CAA "Head of Hearts" told me "We don't know what is wrong but your heart is non-standard so we cannot give you back your full licence". I asked "How bad is it?" and he replied "Well, you might have two years or you might have a fortnight, difficult to say!" That was about 30 years ago and I'm here and the Heart Specialist died of a heart attack 5 years after he had seen me! When I told my wife about the irregular heart beat under stress or excitement her reply was "I could have told them that. You have always been like that!"

After my wife had died in 1997 I was concerned that nobody now knew of my strange heart beat and should I have to be attended by Paramedics it might influence their decision and treatment. I went to see my GP and discussed the problem with her and she set in motion another series of tests.

After more poking and prodding the Heart Specialist of the NHS said "There's nothing wrong with your heart – you can go back flying anytime!". Good to hear but at age 66 I was too old for Commercial flying but the CAA had allowed me to have a Licence to fly light aircraft. Fortunately that level of qualification had allowed me to continue flying the aircraft I was asked to use in the work that I had done.

Aircraft Types Flown

9/2/1951	Chipmunk
21/6/1951	Oxford
7/1/1952	Meteor MK7
29/1/1952	Meteor MkIV
17/4/1952	Meteor Mk8
12/6/1952	Balliol
27/11/1952	Varsity
1/1/1953	Valetta
14/11/1953	Anson
24/11/1954	Canberra T4
2/12/1954	Canberra B2
7/2/1956	Valiant
30/6/1958	Victor Mk1
17/5/1961	Victor Mk2
12/8/1963	Provost T1
20/9/1963	Jet Provost
27/11/1963	Gnat T1
30/10/1967	Aircoupe
14/11/1967	Condor
31/5/1968	Cherokee 180
3/6/1968	Cherokee 140
30/8/1968	MFI
5/9/1968	Vagabond
16/9/1968	Beagle 206
22/9/1968	Cessna 172
16/11/1968	Twin Commanche
10/12/1968	DH Rapide DH 89
4/10/1969	Apache
2/5/1970	Boeing 707−436
2/4/1972	Boeing 707−336
18/5/1976	Boeing 720B
29/3/1977	Tiger Moth
7/5/1977	Auster Aiglet
3/6/1977	Fairchild Argus
16/12/1980	Cherokee Arrow
23/6/1981	Piper Tripacer PA22
2/3/1982	Tobago TB10
23/12/1983	Tomahawk
2/6/1982	Stampe

Unlogged
Islander, T33 and Prentice

Glossary of Terms

Airfield Pressure Setting. The atmospheric pressure at the airfield and will show zero altitude when set on an aircraft altimeter setting scale.
Airways. An airway is virtually a "Highway in the Sky" It is a designated route between geographic points with the route limited in a band between heights and a band limiting the distance on either side of the route It is normally marked by radio beacons at start and finish but may have satellite coordinates at either end.
Alert Readiness. This is the state of preparation to fly operationally It may be sitting in the cockpit ready to start the engines with all other preparations done or by sitting in a Crew‑room waiting. Several "Levels" of Readiness were devised to be used as an operation became more imminent.
Alternate. A Diversion Airfield chosen to be used if required.
Artificial Horizon. A flight Instrument showing attitude of the aircraft in pitch and roll.
Asymmetric Flight. Flying with on engine failed on a multi‑engine aircraft.
Beadle Charlie. The call‑sign used to identify me on that day to Air Traffic Control.
Blind Flying Panel. A blind flying panel is on a panel immediately in front of the pilot. It has six instruments and all were originally vacuum powered from a vacuum pump fitted on one of the engines. Originally all were independent of the electrical supply. The six instruments are:‑ Airspeed indicator, altimeter, climb/descent indicator, artificial horizon, turn and slip indicator and a directional gyro.
Bomber Stream. The RAF bombers flew a long, tight, formation in the dark—a 'stream of bombers' flying a common route at the same speed to and from the target, each aircraft being allotted a height band and a time slot in a bomber stream to minimize the risk of formation collision.
Brake Parachute. A large, strong parachute deployed from the rear of the aircraft on landing to help slow down the speed of the aircraft.
Brylcreem. A white hair styling preparation for men. On occasions WWII fighter pilots were known as "Brylcreem Boys" in what today would be called "Celebrity Status".
CFI. CHIEF FLYING INSTRUCTOR: The senior QFI in charge of others.
CGI. Chief Ground Instructor.
City and Guilds. The City and Guilds of London Institute (City & Guilds) is an Internation‑ally respected vocational education organization. It provides courses ranging from basic skills to the highest standards of professional recognition.
Cold War. At the end of WWII the USSR stayed at the boundary of the territory it had won and Europe was divided into East and West, especially Germany. USA and the other Western Powers began to arm themselves against a strike by the USSR into Western Europe. The fact that the USA had atomic weapons prevented any such action and as the USSR gained its own atomic weapons a stalemate ensued until 1989. During this time the UK developed its own nuclear weapons and played a part in the North Atlantic Treaty Organisation (NATO.).
Crew Chief. The person in charge of the Ground‑crew members working on a particular aircraft.
Critical Mach Number. The critical Mach number (Mcr) of an aircraft is the lowest Mach number at which the airflow over some point of the aircraft reaches the speed of sound. At this point the airflow begins to behave differently and has an effect on the handling of the aircraft.

Deflection shot. In combat if you shoot directly at the target the fire will fall behind the aircraft, which has moved on in the time the bullets, or cannon fire, take to get to the aiming point. To hit the target the aiming point has to be ahead of the target on the predicted flightpath, where the aircraft will be when the fire arrives. The amount in front of the target depends on a number of variables but essentially the greater the angle between your aircraft's flight-path and the target path, the further in front you need to aim – greater "deflection".
Dihedral. The upward angle of the wing from the fuselage where they meet.
Dispersal. Originally a remote part of an airfield where aircraft were parked, to reduce the number damaged if an enemy attack hit only part of the airfield.
Diversion Airfield. An airfield suitable for your aircraft to land at if the destination airfield cannot be used.
Drogue. A device rather like a windsock towed a safe distance behind an aircraft for other aircraft to shoot at.
Feathering. Turning the propeller blades on a piston engine end on to the airflow with the objective of reducing aerodynamic drag. This reduced the rudder forces needed to keep the aircraft flying straight.
Flak. Flak is a contraction of the German word "Flugzeugabwehrkanone" meaning "aircraft-defence cannon", a term used in WWII by the RAF for German anti-aircraft fire.
Flak Barrage. Guns grouped together were known as "batteries of guns" and firing together to cover aircraft's path over the target said to put up a "Barrage of Flak".
Flame-out. When a jet engine stopped in the air it was known as a flame-out.
Flare-path. Originally a line or parellel lines of oil burning flares used for take-off and landing at night. Subsequently this became the name for any runway lit by any means, usually electric lights.
Flight Director. This is an additional instrument superimposed on the Attitude Indicator and indicates the attitude demanded to follow a flight-path programmed into the computer system. By matching the aircraft attitude to the director demand, the flight-path can be flown accurately without interpretation by the pilot.
Flight Envelope. The edges of operating limits of height, speed, engine performance and G forces.
G-force. In straight and level flight lift (L) equals weight (W). In a banked turn of 60°, lift equals double the weight (L=2W). The pilot experiences 2G and a doubled weight. The steeper the bank, the greater the G-forces.
Ground Effect. When the aircraft wing is close to the ground the airflow over the wing is affected giving increased lift and reduced drag, from the value of the same forces in clear air at the same airspeed.
Heavy Flak Batteries. Flak is a contraction of the German word "Flugzeugabwehrkanone" meaning "aircraft-defence cannon", a term used in WWII by the RAF for German anti-aircraft fire. Guns grouped together were known as "batteries of guns" and firing together to cover aircraft's path over the target said to put up a "Barrage of Flak". Light Flak was small calibre of short range but Heavy was larger artillery calibre getting to greater heights.
HF. High Frequency radio Originally only used for Morse Code transmissions but later became used for voice transmissions. It has a much greater range than the VHF radio.
IFF. Identification Friend or Foe; a radio device that returned a radar signal, when the aircraft was illuminated, with a code to show that it was "Friendly" and not an enemy aircraft.

Instrument Landing System (ILS). This consisted basically of two radio beams. A Localiser radio beam to align the aircraft with the runway and a Glide−path radio beam to show the correct approach path on the descent to the runway for landing.

Instrument let-down. A designated flight path for the aircraft to follow when descending to an airfield runway ready for landing. This often used to begin overhead the airfield and in− volved flying away from the runway before turning back to complete the descent and landing.

Instrument panel. The panel in front of the pilots holding the instruments for flying in cloud. The six instruments are:− Airspeed indicator, altimeter, climb/descent indicator, artifi− cial horizon, turn and slip indicator and a directional gyro.

Intercom. Used for personal communication between crew members by their headsets.

Iron Curtain. The Iron Curtain was what Churchill called the physical boundary dividing Europe into two separate areas from the end of World War II in 1945 until the end of the Cold War in 1991.

Jet-stream. This is a band of very strong winds that is found along the boundary between warm and cold air, and sits just below the stratosphere. Speeds of the winds can reach up to 200 miles per hour and these jet−streams have a marked affect on weather systems and airliner flight paths.

Landing Flare. This is the reduction in rate of descent from the final part of the approach path to a gentle touchdown with zero rate of descent.

Link Trainer. The original Link Trainer came into use in the 1930s to teach student pilots how to fly by instruments.

It looked like an aircraft from the outside, with short wings and fuselage with a hood over the cockpit. This was all mounted on a single universal joint and was tilted in pitch and roll by a set of bellows as the pilot moved the controls. With the hood closed the movements were just enough to disorientate the student so they had to rely on the instruments to perform the flight pattern.

Mach Number. Mach 1 is the speed of sound in a particular environment. At speeds of an aircraft less than the speed of sound a decimal is used to show the speed – 0.95 is close to the speed of sound, 0.75 not as close to the speed of sound.

Master Bomber. The highly dangerous role of "Master Bomber" was introduced as a sort of master of ceremonies, the appointed Pathfinder (usually a highly experienced senior Officer) circling the target and broadcasting instructions to both Pathfinders and Main Force aircraft, correcting aiming points and generally coordinating the attack.

Morse Code. A method developed by Samuel Morse originally used for transmitting messages on the electric telegraph using an alphabet and numbers represented by sets of written dots and dashes. Later it was used extensively by the military using radio signals or flashing lights. For many years extensively used for long distance High Frequency radio communication.

OC Flying. Officer Commanding Flying.

OCU. Operational Conversion Unit: where crews trained to fly a new aircraft or for a new role.

PAR. Precision Approach Radar This is a radar system that shows the Ground Controller where an aircraft on the approach is in relation to the Centre−line and Glide−path to a run− way. He can then give the pilot guidance on how to maintain a stable approach to the runway.

Pathfinder. The WWII elite force of Bomber Command who went in ahead of the Bomber Stream and marked the target with flares for the Main Force to aim at.

Pitot Head. Measuring instrument consisting of a combined Pitot tube and static tube that measures total and static pressure; used in aircraft to measure airspeed.

Pitot/Static System. The pitot–static system of instruments senses the change in air pressure. It is possible by measuring pressures or pressure differences to estimate the speed and altitude. These pressures are used from either the static port (static pressure) or the pitot tube (pitot pressure). The static pressure is used by all instruments, while the pitot pressure is only for airspeed.
QFI: A Flying Instructor trained at the RAF Central Flying School, designated Qualified Flying Instructor.
Queen Fox Easy. The phonetics used to designate the letters of the alphabet; Q, F, and E. QFE was part of what was known as the "Q" Code where groups of three letters, always beginning with Q, were used to pass complex messages. QFE gives the atmospheric pressure currently at the airfield. The bottom line is: when you set this pressure on the altimeter it reads zero so when you take–off it will show height above the airfield.
Ranger flight. The name given to overseas flights by individual aircraft to give crews navigational and environmental experience.
Readiness. This is the state of preparation to fly operationally. It may be sitting in the cockpit ready to start the engines with all other preparations done or sitting in a Crew–room waiting. Several "Levels" of Readiness were devised to be used as an operation became more imminent.
Roger. An abbreviation used in a radio message meaning "Message received and understood".
SAM. A surface–to–air missile (SAM), or ground–to–air missile (GTAM), is a missile designed to be launched from the ground to destroy aircraft or other missiles.
Scramble. The moment when Readiness turns to Operation and crews run to their aircraft and take off.
Stall. The airflow that gives lift from the wing flows smoothly over the upper surface of the wing and breaks away into turbulent air at the trailing–edge(back of the wing). As the angle between the airflow and the wing increases when the nose of the aircraft moves up, the lift is increased and the point at which the turbulent air that detaches moves towards the leading edge. As this process continues there is eventually not enough lift to overcome the aircraft weight and the aircraft will drop as it enters a condition known as a stall.
Stall Buffet. When the aircraft approaches the stall, and loses lift, the airflow across the upper cambered surface of the wing ceases to flow smoothly. The airflow breaks away from the wing surface and becomes turbulent. If the turbulent air from the wing then flows across the horizontal stabilizer on the tail, vibration of the stick, and sometimes the tail itself, called buffet results.
Target Indicator. A flare dropped by a Pathfinder aircraft to mark the general area of the target.
Target Marker. A flare dropped by a Pathfinder aircraft on the target for the other bombers to aim at. If not right on target the Master Bomber will give an offset point from the marker to aim at.
Test Pilot. Is a pilot who flies new and modified aircraft in specific manoeuvres, known as flight test techniques, allowing the results to be measured and the design to be evaluated.
Transponder. A modern version of the IFF system from WWII, now used every day by modern airliners.
Trim. Secondary flying controls to enable the pilot finer control but mainly to ease the pressure on the controls held by the pilot. The most commonly available trim is on the elevator operated by a wheel or other device, so that the pilot does not have to maintain constant backward or forward pressure to hold a steady pitch attitude. Other types of trim, for rudder and ailerons, are common even on smaller aircraft.

Undercarriage Flag. If there was one instrument the pilot could be relied upon to be looking at on the approach to landing it was the airspeed indicator. On that instrument a small hatched indicator would appear if the speed reduced towards the landing speed and the undercarriage was not fully lowered.

V-Force. Was the name given to the UK bombers armed with nuclear weapons in the Cold War. "V" because the bombers were called Valiant, Vulcan and Victor.

VHF. Very High Frequency radio. Normally used for voice communication known as RT(Radio Telephony) and has only a comparatively short range.

Vital Actions. The checks done by a pilot before take off or landing to ensure that the aircraft configuration was correct. They were done to a mnemonic for each occasion which fitted all aircraft types at the time.

Wireless. Original name for radio broadcasts for entertainment and communication. Later generally used as a term to differentiate from signals sent in Morse Code and voice communication, which was known as RT or Radio Transmissions.

AUTHOR'S QUALIFICATIONS AND EXPERIENCE

As Peer Recognition I was awarded:
Queen's Commendation for Valuable Service in the Air.
Made a Fellow of the Royal Aeronautical Society.
As an Upper Freeman of the Guild of Air Pilots and Air Navigators made a Liveryman and Freeman of the City of London.
Chairman of the British Association of Aviation Consultants.
Made Honorary Member of the British Association of Aviation Consultants.
Recognition by the Flight Safety Foundation
A letter of appreciation for my services to aviation safety
Flying Qualifications and Experience;
In the RAF:
Fighter Pilot, Bomber Pilot, Staff Pilot and Qualified Flying Instructor.

In Civil Flying:
Held an Airline Transport Pilots Licence and a Flight Navigators Licence.
Licensed as an Examiner of Flight Navigators.
Civil Flying Instructor Group "A" and Examiner for IMC Ratings.

Professional:
For British Airline Pilots Association (BALPA) served on the Course Failure Working Party and the Concord Evaluation Team.
As an Aviation Consultant, worked for UK Civil Aviation Authority at the Royal Air Force Institute of Aviation Medicine (RAFIAM), Psychology Department. Involved in experimental flying for measuring performance reduction of pilots due to sleep loss.
Consultant on Confidential Human Factors Incident Reporting Program (CHIRP) at the RAFIAM.
Consultant to Technical University of Berlin for EUCARE, the European project similar to CHIRP in the UK.
Served on the Human Factors Group and the Flight Operations Group of the Royal Aeronautical Society.
Served as Clerk to the Guild of Air Pilots and Air Navigators.
Acted as Expert Witness for a number of Court Actions.
Broadcaster on International TV and Radio, on Aviation Safety, and now Author.